S0-CLE-574

Grass Roots

RELEASE

Grass

Roots

by ROSCOE C. MARTIN

ST. JOSEPH'S UNIVERSITY

JS331.M29 1978   STX

Grass roots /

RELEASED

3 9353 00135 8967

JS
331
.M29
1978

208558

GREENWOOD PRESS, PUBLISHERS
WESTPORT, CONNECTICUT

Library of Congress Cataloging in Publication Data

Martin, Roscoe Coleman, 1903-1972.
  Grass roots.

    Reprint of the 1964 ed. published by the University
of Alabama Press, University, Ala.
    Lectures given in 1955 before graduate students of
the Southern Regional Training Program in Public
Administration and members of the faculty of political
science of the University of Alabama.
    Includes index.
    1. Local government—United States.   I.   Title.
[JS331.M29 1978]   352.073   78-5058
ISBN 0-8371-9347-8

Copyright 1957 by University of Alabama Press
University, Alabama

Reprinted with the permission of University of
Alabama Press

Reprinted in 1978 by Greenwood Press, Inc.
51 Riverside Avenue, Westport, CT. 06880

Printed in the United States of America

10 9 8 7 6 5 4 3 2 1

Preface

THESE ESSAYS are eleventh in line in a series which began in 1944. Like its predecessors in the "Alabama Series," this volume comprises the annual fall lectures—this time for 1955—given before the graduate students of the Southern Regional Training Program in Public Administration and the members of the faculty of political science of the University of Alabama. There is one exception to be noted: a fifth lecture, delivered before a joint meeting of the two University groups and the Alabama chapter of the American Society for Public Administration, did not contribute directly to the major theme developed by the series and so is omitted.

Others have spoken of the generous hospitality accorded them by the people at Alabama, and of the scholarship they found in ferment there. I need say only that my own reception was nonetheless warm because of my recent conversion from consumer to producer, and that the intellectual atmosphere was as exhilarating as I remembered it to be. I enjoyed to the utmost my week at the University of Alabama. I am grateful to York Willbern for the invitation which made it possible, and to him and his colleagues, student as well as faculty, for the stimulation which made it rewarding.

The lectures were prepared during a semester's research leave from Syracuse University. I wish to express to the officers of that institution my appreciation of their consideration.

ROSCOE C. MARTIN

Syracuse, New York

Contents

i The Grass-roots Concept

In september of 1935 Governor Alf Landon of Kansas, with the courage and imagination that a year later were to win him fame, spoke out in opposition to county and township consolidation on the ground that he favored continuation of " . . . democracy at the grass roots." Ten years later Harold D. Smith, then Director of the United States Budget, observed that "there are dynamics at the grass roots. These dynamics should be harnessed and used for the preservation and extension of democracy." In 1949 V. O. Key wrote that "the New Deal . . . reached down to the grass roots and actually had some bearing on the course of human events." To *Newsweek*, the voters of the Ninth Congressional District of Wisconsin uttered a "grass-roots warning" in electing Lester Johnson (Democrat) to the House of Representatives in 1953. On March 17, 1955, the *Register-Guard* of Eugene, Oregon, editorialized to the effect that "every man is a grass root in the mind of the Foreign Policy Association, [whose program is] based on the theory that people do count." For one observer, the recent White House Conference on Education lost its intended character when the educational "pros" wrested control from "the average delegates from grass-roots America." To leave no blade unturned, Mr. Herbert Edward Read lately published four lectures under the title *The Grass Roots of Art*. It is obvious that the term "grass roots" is used by a wide variety of individuals in an equally wide variety of senses.

But if grass roots lends itself to chance and vagrant employment by some, it is put to purposeful use by others. To David E. Lilienthal, for example, it means a method of operation by which the Tennessee Valley Authority on the one hand has shared responsibility with the common people of the region and on the other hand has enlisted their support in the pursuit of numerous Valley-wide enterprises. In a best-seller of its class,* Lilienthal has described at length and with obvious enthusiasm the involvement of the people of the Valley in TVA's manifold programs. The author's point of view is well summarized in the following passage: "I find it impossible to comprehend how democracy can be a living reality if people are remote from their government and in their daily lives are not made a part of it, or if the control and direction of making a living—industry, farming, the distribution of goods—is too far removed from the stream of life and the local community." The spirit of his argument is caught in such phrases as "the day-to-day accountability of working partner to working partner," "an emigration of talent to the grass roots," "decentralized grass-roots administration," "the self-education of citizens," and "the habit of working together." Here is a vigorous explication of the grass-roots concept, in terms both of the time-worn administrative desiderata of economy and efficiency and of the more broadly democratic values which are summed up in the term citizen participation. The attacks upon Mr. Lilienthal's major thesis on technical grounds by both an academic sociologist and a former New Deal stalwart in no way affect his credibility as spokesman for a philosophy which to him means something specific, concrete, and immediate.

* *TVA: Democracy on the March* (New York: Harper & Brothers, 1944, revised 1953).

An analysis of grass roots in its more responsible employment will suggest that it has at least five significant facets. First, it is usually employed in connection with government. In the general area of public affairs it may be used in reference to administrative decentralization, for example, or to the representativeness of the legislative organ, or to political action "at the branchhead." Obviously not all such references have scientific validity or content; but we will pass by this demurrer for the present in favor of a general bounding of the term.

Second, the concept appears normally to have a geographical import. In this sense, a place which partakes of the grass roots is non-metropolitan, even non-urban, in character. A well-known political writer recently equated the rural "wool hat" voter with "grassroots politics." Another observer of the current scene commented that "to find the grass roots sentiment we have to go where the grass grows." It should be added quickly that identification, in this respect in particular, is likely to depend upon point of view; Wichita, Kansas, clearly is grass roots when viewed from New York City, while seen from Medicine Lodge it is just as clearly a metropolitan center. Whether the view is upward or downward, then, is relevant in identifying a grass-roots locus. So is distance; distance from the person doing the identifying, but more especially distance from Washington, since nobody, so far as a fairly careful search reveals, ever attributed the quality of grass roots to that city. It may be proposed as an early law that the grass-roots character of a given phenomenon (place, event, program) increases directly with the square of its distance from Washington.

Third, grass roots is frequently employed to symbolize a spirit of community independence. The basic problems of government, the argument goes, are local in character, and should be dealt with by local initiative. Stated positively, this view leads logically to the doctrine of local self-government and home-rule; it results in the requirement of local residence for candidates for public office, in support of the principle of "home town boys for home town jobs," and in a provincial approach to public affairs. Carried farther, it eventuates in the doctrines of states' rights and isolationism, and, ultimately, in "interposition," nullification, and secession. Most grass-roots devotees, of course, stop far short of any such extreme position, and are content generally to rest their case on the principle of local control of local affairs. Even a moderate stand, however, is accompanied often by suspicion of foreign (that is, non-local) forces and by fear of outside interference and control.

Fourth, in one of its important aspects the term has a personal or individual meaning. Thus a view held by an individual is *ipso facto* a grass-roots view, an expression of personal opinion a grass-roots judgment. In this sense, the concept is not limited geographically but has application wherever people are found, although its validity is always greater when it is applied to a rural setting. In this sense, too, grass roots is an expression of belief in the worth of the individual, of confidence in personal judgment.

Fifth, and as a direct corollary to the above, grass roots is almost invariably equated with democracy. Thus it is never said that Franco enjoys grass-roots support among the Spanish people, or that the Japanese Empire rests upon a broad grass-roots foundation. Grass roots would appear to be a peculiarly American phenomenon ultimately connected with the expression of popular judgment on public questions. It is in fact an important symbol of American democracy. It provides, in a sense, a court of last appeal, since in democratic doctrine there is no tribunal above or beyond the people. In final analysis, grass roots serves as a fundamental article of the democratic faith, for it carries the indelible impression of the sovereign individual. Again a witness is found in Lilienthal, who builds the bridge from grass-roots individualism to grass-roots democracy in these words: "To see each citizen as a 'human being' is far easier at the grass roots. That is where more of the functions of . . . government should be exercised."

Given this kind of content, it is not strange that the grass-roots concept is invoked with confidence in support of manifold causes, or that it is treated almost universally with a respect bordering on reverence. Those who reside at the grass roots are reckoned to be substantial, virtuous folk, their motives high and their judgment sound. One who rejects or ignores a grass-roots incantation does so at his peril, for the public mind does not entertain the alternative of grass-roots fallibility. *In hoc signo vinces* was not devised for the grass-roots talisman, but it might have been.

Philosophical Foundation

It is not difficult to account for America's preoccupation with grass roots, for it rests squarely upon doctrine which has been central to our thinking and which for the most part has guided the course of the Republic almost from the beginning. The most persuasive spokesman of the new-born democracy in its early days was Thomas Jefferson — de Tocqueville called him ". . . the most powerful advocate democracy has ever had."

It is important to note first of all that Jefferson was an agrarian. He held the agricultural way of life to be good in itself, and productive of virtue in those who followed it. "I think our governments will remain virtuous for many centuries," he wrote, "as long as they are chiefly agricultural; and this will be as long as there shall be vacant lands in any part of America." His confidence in those who practiced agriculture was equaled only by his distrust of the "mobs of great cities," which he viewed as "pestilential to the morals, health and liberties of man."

Not only was Jefferson an agrarian; he was an agrarian with a small "a": he was not an Agriculturist but a farmer, in his affections if not in life. A large land-holder himself and a "country gentleman" by the standards of the day, he nevertheless rejected the physio-cratic emphasis on large estates in favor of accent on small, individual holdings. Gentlemen planters of the tidewater were rich in acres but few in number; the landholder who commanded Jefferson's respect was the small farmer of the Piedmont and the frontier who owned and worked his own plot. The great mass of small farmer-owners provided the bedrock of the Jef-fersonian social and economic system.

But if Jefferson was a staunch agrarian, he was at the same time the arch-advocate of democracy. His es-pousal of the cause of the common man rested upon both philosophical and practical considerations. As a philosopher, Jefferson accepted as basic premises the essential dignity of man and his equality in all things moral and spiritual; he accorded man "certain inalien-able rights" as man. As a politician, Jefferson knew instinctively where the political power lay, where in-deed it must lie, in the new commonwealth. It lay not with the patroons along the Hudson but with the westerners who rallied around Herkimer at Oriskany, not with the plantation owners of the tideland but with the frontiersmen who fought at King's Mountain. Almost all Americans were farmers in Jefferson's day, and almost all farmers were small farmers.

It was at the confluence of agrarianism and democracy, then, that Jefferson took his stand. His polity, could he have brought it to pass, would have been a rural democracy in which the small farmers would have exercised complete control. "The article . . . nearest my heart," he wrote in 1816, "is the division of counties into wards.* These will be pure and elementary republics, the sum of all of which, taken together, composes the State, and will make of the whole a true Democracy as to the business of the wards, which is that of nearest and daily concern."

Jefferson's emphasis upon agriculture was so great that at one time he would have excluded manufactures as inimical to the public interest. In his later years, in recognition of changing times and new needs, he made grudging concession to the utility of American manufactures, though the cities to which they gave rise never commanded more than reluctant sufferance. He noted with approval that commercial cities, though they made a great deal of noise through control of the newspapers, had little influence in the government. For Thomas Jefferson, it remained true to the end that "those who labor in the earth are the chosen people of God."

Jefferson's ideal of an agricultural republic resting upon a small farmer-owner class has exerted a profound influence upon the course of American democratic thought. The many and fundamental changes in our way of life—those accompanying the technological revolution, for example, and those attendant upon America's emergence as a world power—have served only partially to release the national mind from the straightjacket of agrarian thinking. The principal stronghold of agricultural democracy today is found in the United States Department of Agriculture, which has identified

* In terms familiar to our ears, Jefferson's "wards" would be rendered as "towns" or "townships."

the "family-size, owner-operated farm" as a major objective and which recognizes the rural community as the basic unit for democratic action. Some years ago the Secretary of Agriculture acclaimed Jefferson as the progenitor of departmental policy in some of its fundamental aspects. Thus, a student of the subject was moved to conclude, have Jefferson's principles lived on " . . . to inspire the framers of modern agricultural policy and color the thoughts of Americans when they turn their minds to rural life."

In summary, the Jeffersonian legacy for modern America consists in two major propositions. The first, resting upon a fundamental conviction of the essential dignity of man and worth of the individual, is that government draws its authority from the consent of the governed. This proposition finds expression in an all-but-unanimous homage to democracy, to which virtually all Americans pay at least lip service. The second is that the virtues of loyalty, prudence, frugality, and indeed common honesty are more generously distributed among rural than among urban dwellers. This proposition, while perhaps not so widely accepted as the first, nevertheless finds ready and ardent sponsorship. Jefferson's dogmas about the "mobs of the cities" and the "chosen people" of the countryside die hard.

Institutions and Grass Roots

Grass roots emerges therefore, on examination, as something more than a catch-phrase at the tip of every writer's pen and every speaker's tongue. It has to do with a fundamental aspect of the practice of democracy in America. It concerns the individual citizen, and more particularly, in view of the continuing strength of the Jeffersonian tradition, the rural citizen, in his contacts with public affairs. It is involved with rural democracy

—with little democracy and little government, and with the many organizations and institutions established by the people to make their voice heard in the governance of their affairs.

Chief among these, of course, are the institutions of government itself, and these will receive proper attention in due course. Meanwhile, it is necessary to bear in mind that democracy manifests itself not alone through the agencies of government, but through a variety of other channels as well. It is a truism that Americans are the world's greatest joiners of organizations. De Tocqueville observed this tendency, which was already emerging as a national trait when he wrote 130 years ago. "In no country in the world," he said, "has the principle of association been more successfully used or applied to a greater multitude of objects than in America. Besides the permanent associations which are established by law under the names of townships, cities, and counties, a vast number of others are formed and maintained by the agency of private individuals. . . . There is no end to which the human will despairs of attaining through the combined power of individuals united into a society." Of these societies there are now many thousands, more than have ever been tallied in a reliable census. They range from local organizations to state associations to national federations; they run in membership from as few as a dozen in the case of a single local club to some millions in a few of the larger federations; they range in interests from the purely social and fraternal to the professional and the occupational, in programs from the operation of a local pool hall to a drive to raise the tariff on Swiss watches, in public consequence from the small-town club which seeks only to serve the needs or the pleasures of its immediate members to the national organization whose governing body constitutes something approaching an economic parliament, with a direct and demonstrable effect on national public policy.

It would, of course, prove wholly futile to attempt to analyze this multitude of "societies" here. Fortunately, it is not necessary to make the attempt, if only because the great majority of them have little effect on the course of public affairs. This does not mean that the Thursday Afternoon Reading Club may not occasionally pass a resolution excoriating Mr. Khrushchev, or the local Parent-Teacher Association a resolution concerning atomic warfare; it does mean that such resolutions are generally recognized not to be in the main channel of the purposes of these organizations which, lacking tradition, strength, and lateral support outside their special fields, expect such pronouncements to be ignored—as indeed they are normally, notwithstanding their unmistakably grass-roots flavor. What can be done with profit is to summarize briefly a few of the principal organizations in three major fields which, though in the private sector, have definite interests and conduct active programs in the area of public affairs.

In the domain of business, the American propensity for organization finds full expression. Here are encountered associations of retail merchants, truckers, druggists, laundrymen, airlines, jewelers, sales executives, railroads—the list is endless, and is brought to a conclusion only by observing that there is a local organization, the chamber of commerce, which comes nearer representing all local businesses than any other. The individual chambers of commerce are associated together in state chambers and finally in the United States Chamber of Commerce, which represents approximately 2,300 local chambers and 20,000 individual members. On the industrial side there is the National

Association of Manufacturers, which has a membership estimated at 15,000 firms. Both NAM and the Chamber of Commerce maintain headquarters in Washington (as do many other national business organizations), where they keep a jealous eye on developments which affect industry and business. Many of the state chambers maintain headquarters in the state capitals, where they perform for their individual members services comparable to those done by the national organization in Washington.

The labor unions of America have almost seventeen million members. The overwhelming majority of these belong to the recently merged A. F. of L.-C. I. O., although the United Mine Workers, the Railroad Brotherhoods, and numerous other independent unions account for 2.5 million. A recent census reported approximately 197 national or international unions with an estimated 60,000 to 70,000 locals. In addition, there were 795 city central organizations and 50 state federations maintained by the A. F. of L., and 243 city, county, and district councils, along with 39 industrial councils, maintained by the C. I. O. Like the United States Chamber of Commerce and the NAM, the larger unions maintain permanent headquarters in Washington; and like their business counterparts they are ceaselessly engaged in behalf of their membership.

Agriculture finds its institutional representatives in three principal organizations. The first of these, the Grange, goes back almost ninety years. Its program emphasizes social, recreational, fraternal, and educational activities, though it does not hesitate to make its views known on public issues. The second important farmers' organization is the National Farmers Union, a vigorous association representing more than 300,000 farm families whose principal concern is the "little farmer." By all odds the most effective of the agri-

cultural organizations, in terms of its influence on
public affairs, is the American Farm Bureau Federa-
tion, which claims a membership of some 1.25 million
farm families. The AFBF has a very close tie-in with
the United States Department of Agriculture and the
land grant colleges. It represents principally (though
not exclusively) the large farmer, and its primary concern is to make of agriculture a successful commercial
enterprise. It has comparatively few members among
the small farmer class, and some have charged that
it is not much concerned with the lot of the little
farmer; it is indicative that the Farm Bureau rejected
the Farm Security Administration, a unit within the
Department of Agriculture which was set up with the
welfare of the small farmer in mind.

These several organizations have been highly effective in gaining special consideration for their respective
constituents, and they are integral and important elements in America's unofficial hierarchy of economic
representation. Their significance for the grass-roots
concept, however, is very limited, and for two principal
reasons. In the first place, most such organizations do
not have effective operating units in the rural areas—
they were not "branchhead" associations in their origins,
and their grass-roots contacts for the most part are
tenuous, indirect, and uncertain. For most of them, the
traffic from the top downward is much heavier than
that from the bottom upward.

In the second place, such organizations are not, generally speaking, democratic in their methods or their
organization. A labor union official has written a very
perceptive article on anti-democratic tendencies in the
unions.* He points out that in its early days a union's
administration will be strictly amateur. Elected by the

* Will Herberg, "Bureaucracy and Democracy in Labor Unions,"
The Antioch Review, III (Fall, 1943), 405-417.

membership in open meeting, the executive board directs the affairs of the organization in an informal, personal, friendly way. As the union increases in size, however, as it launches upon new activities, as it gains in power and position, as it augments its resources, full-time functionaries take over. "The Office" assumes more and more power, with the consequence that less and less authority is left to the membership in meeting. The Office comes to have primary responsibility for the program, which it proposes to the membership not for public debate but for approval; and gradually function and functionary tend to become identified as one. In the process of amalgamation (which is none the less effective because subtle), The Office assumes a sacrosanct character; losing its sense of responsibility to its principal, it grows impatient of membership questions and criticisms, which it interprets as being aimed at The Program and so as savoring of either subversion or sabotage. At this point The Office has become a bureaucracy, and hope of self-government has vanished.

In this development, the author relates, (a) the membership loses virtually all power save that of ratification, excepting in the event of a dramatic division; (b) self-government becomes so limited as to suffer virtual extinction; (c) control passes to the administration, that is, to the bureaucracy; (d) the union's government falls into the ways of power politics; (e) means come to be subordinated to ends; and (f) opposition is rooted out and destroyed, with the civil rights of the membership suffering severe restrictions in the process. The worst of all this is that the membership not only accepts these developments placidly but embraces them positively, so long as the bureaucracy produces results and there is no schism sufficiently serious to threaten its overthrow. "Even in democratic unions," Mr. Herberg concludes, "the effective power of top officials is greater, their

grip tighter, their tenure more secure, their conduct in
office less open to public criticism and control, than
is commonly the case in our federal or state governments in normal times."

The Herberg article was penned not in criticism
of the unions but in explanation of a tendency which
besets all organizations. Some are able to stem the
anti-democratic reaction and keep control close to the
people, but most fall victim to the process of arterio-
sclerosis described above. The disease attacks without
discrimination organizations in business, in labor, in
agriculture—and in government. Silent renunciation
of the ebullient democracy of youth and equally silent
embrace of the defensive and testy bureaucracy of ad-
vancing years, size, and opulence are companion and
constant threats to organizations everywhere.

What, then, of grass roots and its practice? The answer is clear: local democracy generally does not prevail
in private organizations, great or small, not even in
those whose programs carry them vigorously into the
field of public affairs. The "little man," the individual
citizen whose principal preoccupation is to make a
living for himself and his family, is almost never inti-
mately involved in the trade-industrial-occupational organizations, and frequently he is not involved at all.
Such organizations have little or nothing to do with
the small communities or with those who dwell there.
The man who makes a living on his farm, the village
craftsman, in short the little people generally, are members of the great amorphous public which is not represented by economic or other special-interest groups. All
such must place their dependence upon public representatives, upon government, otherwise their cause will
not be heard.

The "New Democracy" of Agriculture

The United States Department of Agriculture has been identified as chief among the latter-day protagonists of the Jeffersonian concept of an agrarian democracy. It may now be further identified as chief exemplar as well, since through its multiform system of administrative and advisory committees it has striven valiantly to bring one phase of government to the doorstep of the farmer. As early as 1939 M. L. Wilson, then Under Secretary of Agriculture, brought out a volume which had as a persistent undertone the "new democracy of Agriculture."* "The signs of the times," Mr. Wilson concluded, "point to a great new surge of agricultural democracy. . . ."

The new manifestation of agrarian democracy took the form of a complicated system of citizen committees which were related to the various substantive programs of the department. There were community, county, and state committees which operated in conjunction with the Agricultural Adjustment Administration and its successors; community, county, and state land-use committees; a veritable army of volunteer leaders in agricultural extension education; boards of directors of national farm-loan associations; production credit associations and farmers' co-operatives (Farm Credit Administration); a variety of committees connected

* M. L. Wilson, *Democracy Has Roots* (New York: Carrick and Evans, 1939). In the discussion which follows the past tense is used in describing and evaluating Agriculture's "New Democracy." This is because the system was embraced with more fervor in its early days than now, and further because there is more information available for the earlier period than for the later. It is necessary to note that the citizen committees continue in operation substantially as described here, if with diminished conviction that they herald the beginning of a new day of democracy in agriculture.

with the Farm Security Administration; district advisory boards for the Grazing Service; boards of directors of REA co-operatives; and boards of supervisors
of soil conservation districts. At the same time, the
TVA employed a system of community committees and
demonstration farmers in connection with its fertilizer
test-demonstration program. The nature and extent of
the devices for citizen involvement are suggested by a
tabulation made in 1940. Carleton R. Ball in that year
found the following numbers of citizens serving in the
capacities indicated: *

Name of Citizen Groups	Number of Members
AAA: local committees	135,591
County land-use committees	72,000
Extension Service: volunteer program leaders	586,600
FCA: association directors and committees	36,574
FSA: local committees	26,753
Grazing Service: district advisory boards	547
REA: association directors	4,900
Soil Conservation district supervisors	855
TVA: committees and test-demonstrators	29,035
Total	892,855

These lay program participants varied greatly in
composition and character. Some were individual citizens who served on a volunteer basis; others took the
form of boards or committees. Among the latter,
method of appointment or election, term, and compensation were in no wise uniform. Powers and duties
likewise varied greatly. Some units were administrative,
some representative; some had some power of decision,
some were deliberative and advisory only. On closer
view, then, the system of citizen participation appears

* "Citizens Help Plan and Operate Action Programs," *Land Policy
Review*, III, No. 2 (March-April, 1940), 19-27.

to have been worked out program by program, with each operating agency devising its own plan in general harmony with departmental policy.

The advantages which the system was expected to achieve were several. First, it was thought, it would lead to increased popular understanding of program purposes and procedures, and public (more accurately, client) education therefore received emphasis. Second, broader understanding was expected to result in wider farmer participation and greater local initiative. Third, this in turn would lead to an increased measure of local democracy; indeed the developments traced, it was assumed, would themselves signalize the advent of a more vigorous and more meaningful rural democracy. Fourth, the chasm separating the rural community from Washington would be bridged, and by a two-lane way: not only would the farmers and their needs be brought closer to the national capital, but the officials in Washington would achieve a direct and realistic grasp of the problems with which they were required to deal. Fifth, this would result in the improved administration of agricultural affairs, through more intimate mutual acquaintance of officials and clients, through cliental involvement, and through the consequent "humanization" of the administrative system. Sixth, the glaring discrepancies between democratic ideal and operating reality, between vigorous doctrine and tardy performance, would be minimized if not, in time, eradicated outright.

Opinion differs widely on the question of how well the system of citizen participation worked in practice. Secretary Brannan called it ". . . the most representative, efficient and democratic mechanism that has ever been developed for the administration of farm programs," and Under Secretary Wilson's estimate was equally high. An unofficial observer identified the soil conservation district as the "elementary republic" of Thomas Jefferson, and spoke favorably of the system of "local self-government" which he found there. Others have been less generous in their appraisals. One critic characterized the farmer committee system of the Agricultural Adjustment Administration-Agricultural Adjustment Agency-Production and Marketing Administration as anything but brilliant in its achievements. Another concluded that the committee scheme of the Farm Security Administration failed to achieve its major objectives. Yet another took issue with the generally favorable evaluation of TVA's program of citizen participation.

The major general criticisms leveled at Agriculture's "new democracy" may be summarized thus:

1. The system did not represent a genuine attempt to decentralize in any important respect the process by which significant decisions were made. The purpose rather was merely to involve citizens in substantive programs in order to facilitate execution. The scheme therefore sailed under false colors, for its ostensible purpose was not its real purpose.

2. In operation, the plan failed in its announced intention of democratizing government (or administration). First, farmers eligible to attend meetings and cast ballots did not do so in any considerable numbers after the new wore off. Second, the familiar tendency toward bureaucracy, in the habitual re-election of certain "recognized leaders," was widely noted. Third, farmer participation did not penetrate to the grass *roots* but stopped off with the grass *tops*. The machinery of citizen participation too often was left in the hands of the County (Extension) Agent, who turned to the farmer he worked with and knew best, that is to say, the Farm Bureau farmer. The little farmer was left to weed his corn without molestation by the democratizers.

3. In so far as the system called for administrative decentralization, it affected adversely the legal and still-responsible system of administration. This it accomplished through unwarranted dispersion of responsibility and authority. Further, it vested local administrative duties in persons ill-equipped through training or experience to assume them.

4. Ineffective communication, resulting in part from the casual and sporadic character of local contacts, in part from the novelty and complexity of the scheme, kept the participants in a state of uncertainty, not to say confusion, regarding program aims and expectations.

5. Whatever the validity of these arguments—and opinion varied sharply from issue to issue—it is clear enough that the "new democracy" resulted in a significant fragmentation of government. For one thing, the citizen's interest and attention were divided, in that he was required to concentrate upon farm problems instead of trying to view the local scene whole. For another, the strictly agricultural approach to agriculture's problems had (and has) unfortunate effects on the government in Washington, setting the Congress (as the champion of agrarian rights) and the President (as the spokesman of all the people) against each other in an unnatural and unnecessary class struggle. For still another, and as a corollary, it encouraged a separatist at the expense of a general or inclusive approach to the problems of government.

It is the last point which condemns the "new democracy" of the Department of Agriculture, regardless of the merits of the remainder of the argument. Agriculture's solution to the problem of strengthening local democracy was a plan for citizen participation which emphasized farm problems to the virtual exclusion of all others. This system did not prove satisfactory because it resulted in a warped or biased citizenry—to the extent, at least, that it was successful in its avowed purpose. A broad and general grasp of the affairs of government does not flow from immersion in the technical aspects of one particular program.

The "new democracy" exacerbated the relations between the whole and its parts by further fragmenting and so further complicating the already highly complex problem of government. Among the requirements for the proper functioning of democracy, including specifically local democracy, is a general rather than a special approach to its problems. Such an emphasis will be found—certainly it is more likely to be found— among the agencies of general government than among the pleaders of the special causes of business, labor, and agriculture. The effective implementation of grass-roots democracy is to be sought, then, through the established agencies of local government.

ii Little Government: General View

GOVERNMENT in the United States by any criterion one may wish to employ is a titantic enterprise. In terms of money, the expenditures of government in 1953 totaled $110.6 billion, revenue $105.5 billion. The public debt stood at just under $300 billion. In terms of public employment, there were 7,232,000 people working for government in October, 1954. What is more, all of these figures were increasing: expenditure was up nine per cent, revenue four per cent, the public debt four per cent from 1952, while public employment had grown by 2.6 per cent since 1953. Government is a great and growing concern of the American people, bigger by far than any individual private undertaking, bigger indeed, in scope and variety of activities and in impact upon the daily lives of the people, than all non-governmental enterprises put together.

The Pattern of Local Government

The functions of government are discharged by a labyrinthine structure whose general contour is indicated by the tabulation on page 22.

Two major facts emerge from even a casual study of the table. First, the machinery of government is overwhelmingly local in character, so far at least as numbers of governmental units are concerned. There are only one federal government and 48 states, leaving

116,694 local units out of a total of 116,743. In other
terms, the story is of course quite a different one. The
federal government spends 70 per cent, state and local
governments 30 per cent of all government expenditures. The federal government collects 71.2 per cent
of all governmental revenues and owes 88.4 per cent
of the public debt; corresponding figures for local
governments are 14.4 per cent and 9.0 per cent, re-
spectively. In financial terms, then, local government
is a minor partner in the total governmental enterprise. The units of government, however, are almost
all local, and they employ more than half of all those
who work for government.

Type of Government	Number of Units		Per Cent Change
	1942	1952	
U. S. Government	1	1	0.0
States	48	48	0.0
Counties	3,050	3,049	—
Municipalities	16,220	16,778	3.4
Townships	18,919	17,202	—9.1
School districts	108,579	67,346	—38.0
Special districts	8,299	12,319	48.4
Total	155,116	116,743	—24.7

Second, the table reveals at once that the machinery
of government is in process of drastic adjustment. Two
units, school districts and townships, declined considerably in numbers from 1942 to 1952, the former by 38
per cent, the latter by 9.0 per cent. Even so, these units
contributed the largest percentages to the total number
of units in 1952; of the whole number, indeed, almost
58 per cent were school districts. Two other units,
municipalities and special districts, increased in numbers from 1942 to 1952, the latter by more than 48 per
cent. The over-all effect nevertheless was a net reduc-

tion, with all units of government decreasing 25 per cent in number in the decade ending with 1952.

Brief reflection will suggest that the 116,694 units of local government are so classified only as a matter of convenience. They are not equally or uniformly "local" even in the eyes of the law, and surely they are not equally local by other criteria. There are 77 counties with a population of 250,000 or more each; these contained 35 per cent of the total county population in 1950. Another 147 with a population between 100,000 and 250,000 each contributed 17 per cent of the total. Thus 224 urban counties, 7.3 per cent of the total number, contained 52 per cent of the total county population. Of the population residing within municipalities in 1952, 46 per cent lived in the 106 cities which had over 100,000 people each. Included here, of course, is New York City, which with 238,000 municipal employees and a monthly payroll of more than $85 million is second only to the federal government as a public employer. Among the school districts, there were 58 with pupil enrollments of more than 25,000 each. These few districts accounted for 19 per cent of all pupils enrolled. The 1,031 largest districts, comprising only 1.5 per cent of the total, enrolled more than 50 per cent of the pupils attending public schools.

Nobody would deny the importance of "big local government," for by almost any standard this is where significant things happen. Not only do public employment and public payrolls center in the cities; industrial payrolls, both wage earner and white collar, concentrate there as well. So do the value of things produced, and wholesale trade, and banking and commerce. Both transportation and communication focus on the cities; the bulk of all railway traffic terminates in urban areas, and half of all railroad passengers either begin or end their travels in a dozen of the largest cities.

Aviation depends in large part on the traffic provided
by the urban areas, which also make intensive use of
the telephone, the telegraph, and the United States
mail. The larger cities are also the cultural centers;
there are found concentrated the radio and television
broadcasting stations, the great dailies, the publishing
houses, the opera, the symphony orchestra, the theater,
the museum, the library.

Truly government has joined America's "bigger and
better" parade, and truly the larger units of urban
government occupy a central position on the local governmental stage. They have within their borders most
of the people, they hire most of the public servants,
they collect and spend most of the public money, they
render most of the services, and their citizens enjoy
most of what are reckoned the good things of life. It
is difficult to avoid the conclusion, on statistical evidence, that 75 per cent of everything that is exciting
takes place in the major population centers.

But a spectrum cannot be described exclusively in
terms of violets and indigos. Moreover, the local government so far described is local only in the sense that
it is not state or federal. It is far removed from the
rural scene, and knows little of the blessings of the
town meeting, where, Emerson believed, ". . . the great
secret of political science was uncovered and the problem solved—how to give every individual his fair weight
in government, without any disorder from numbers."
A tree grows in Brooklyn, but not grass. The centers
of urban life possess few of the attributes commonly
associated with the grass roots.

The other end of the local government spectrum is
found in what may be called "little government," of
which there is a plenitude; for if most government is
local government, most local government, in terms of
numbers of units, is little government. Among the

counties, 254 have less than 5,000 population each, and an additional 508 have between 5,000 and 10,000. Thus 24 per cent of the counties have only 3.5 per cent of the population. These include Loving County, Texas, with 285 people; Alpine County, California, with 323; and Storey County, Nevada, with less than 1,000. Petroleum County, Montana, in 1946 had slightly more than 1,000 people, property valued for tax purposes at less than $1 million, five employees, and an annual payroll of $7,960.

Of the 16,778 municipalities, more than 56 per cent have fewer than 1,000 people each; all together, they account for only 4.3 per cent of the total municipal population. Of all cities, 86 per cent have fewer than 5,000 inhabitants; and they employ only 14 per cent of those in municipal employment. Two incorporated municipalities, Eagle Harbor, Maryland, and Ophir, Colorado, had two inhabitants each in 1940. The 1949 Village Code of Minnesota provides that, in villages between 225 and 450 in population, the salary of the mayor shall be $15 per month, the salary of each trustee $10. Bone Creek, West Virginia, gave way years ago to Auburn, population (1950) 149, because ". . . the word is easy to spell and write." In 1954 it had a mayor and a recorder, both Republicans, and five councilmen, three Republicans and two Democrats.

The 17,202 townships and towns (usually classified under the heading "townships") are found in 22 states. The category includes the towns of the six New England states, New York, and Wisconsin, as well as the townships proper which are concentrated in the Middle West. Employing the terms in their narrower sense, the town is vested with general powers of local government, the township is restricted to a much narrower field of action. The township is predominantly a rural area; 64 per cent of the total number have populations

of less than 1,000 each, and over 86 per cent have less
than 2,500. The ten smallest towns of Vermont have a
combined population of less than 900 persons; the
township of Cedar, South Dakota, has seven people,
and Perkins Plantation, Maine, has nine.

The 67,346 school districts vary greatly in title, in
kind, and in size and scope of activity. Well over 44,000,
or 66 per cent of the total, enroll fewer than fifty
pupils each, and a surprisingly large number have fewer
than five pupils each. There are more than 47,000 one-
teacher schools. Nearly 12,000 districts do not operate
schools at all, but (normally) send their pupils to
neighboring districts. Nebraska ranks first among the
states in number of school districts; over 28 per cent
of its 6,276 districts do not operate schools, while those
that do maintain more than 3,900 one-teacher schools.
Cawley County, Kansas, a few years ago had one school
district employing a teacher where there was not a
single pupil attending school; some other districts had
only one or two pupils; and one-third of all the districts in the county had fewer than six pupils each. It
is only fair to record that great progress has been made
in recent years toward the rationalization of the local
school structure; but the twin goals of a reasonably distributed pupil clientele and a sound tax base for America's public school system still lie in the distant future.

The 12,319 special districts deal with such subjects
as water supply, other utilities, housing, sanitation, soil
conservation, irrigation, flood control, drainage, fire
protection, highways, health and hospitals, and ceme-
teries. Such districts are found in every state, with Illinois leading the field with 1,546 and California second
with 1,390. Illinois statutes provide for 22 types of
special districts, of which 16 types are known to be
in existence. Akin to the special district (sometimes
indeed qualifying to be so classified) is the authority,

which has come into wide use, particularly for the
construction and operation of such revenue-producing
facilities as toll roads and bridges and port and airport
facilities. With a few exceptions, the special district
is characteristically a unit of little government. The
exceptions are important. Thus in 1952 the twelve
largest districts had 35 per cent of all special district
employees, received 38 per cent of all special district
revenue, and owed 28 per cent of all long-term special
district debt. Four districts—the Chicago Transit Authority, the Metropolitan Transit Authority (Massa-
chusetts), the Chicago Park District, and the Port of
New York Authority—overshadowed all others on these
three counts. Preponderantly urban special districts to
the number of less than 17 per cent of the total received
more than 66 per cent of all special district revenue,
accounted for over 72 per cent of all such expenditures,
and owed almost 72 per cent of the total special district
long-term debt. At the other extreme were the districts
which were primarily rural in character. Such were
their number and nature that 71 per cent of all special
districts had no outstanding debt; 74 per cent had total
annual revenue amounting to less than $10,000 each;
and 36 per cent employed no personnel while 82 per
cent had fewer than five employees each.

The increase in number of special districts has been
called the most dramatic current development on the
local government front. It has in truth been striking,
yet it would be a mistake to accept the raw growth
figures at face value without analysis. Such analysis
reveals that four states, through concentration on one
type of district each, contribute twenty per cent of the
total number. These are New York with 816 fire districts, Illinois with 758 drainage districts, Missouri with
582 road-bridge-street improvement districts, and Kansas with 526 cemetery districts. It is significant that 27

states make out without any fire districts at all, 16
without drainage districts, 33 without road districts, and
40 without cemetery districts. A few states thus have
deemed it necessary to establish considerable numbers
of special districts for which other states have found
no need.

Three generalizations regarding the special district
movement would appear useful at this point. First, notwithstanding the rapid multiplication of such units in
urban areas, the growth in the number of special districts is essentially a growth also in grass-roots government. Second, the special district represents a political
response to an unmet (generally a new) need; a special
district is brought into being when there is no existing
unit of government which is able or willing to perform
a needed service. Thus it represents an invention, or
at least an improvisation, in the face of changing conditions. Third, whatever the services performed by the
special district, it contributes powerfully to what one
writer has called "our disintegrating political machinery."

The point has been made that local government, in
terms of number of units, is preponderantly little government. Contemplation of certain trends leads to
speculation whether the proliferation of local government may not be a phenomenon of rural life. The shift
in the urban-rural ratio, in relation to declining numbers of governmental units, is suggestive; for as the
percentage of urban dwellers has increased, the number
of units of government has declined. The hypothesis
to which this observation gives rise is confirmed by
study of the 168 metropolitan areas, as defined by the
Census of 1950. Those areas contained 56 per cent of
the country's total population, but embraced only 14
per cent of the units of local government. Moreover,
there was an inverse relationship between size of metro-

politan area and percentage of local units contained. Thus the five metropolitan areas containing each a city of more than 1,000,000 included 14 per cent of the country's total population, but only 0.6 per cent of the units of local government. Those with central cities between 500,000 and 1,000,000 had 7.8 per cent of the population but only 0.8 per cent of the local units. For those with cities of between 250,000 and 500,000, the percentages were 7.6 and 1.0; for those between 100,000 and 250,000, 9.8 and 2.6; and for those between 50,000 and 100,000, 8.9 and 4.5. Summarizing, it is clear that the larger is the metropolitan area, the smaller is the percentage of local units contained; conversely, the smaller the metropolitan area, the larger the percentage of local units included. In other words, local governments diminish in number as the density of the population increases. This suggests rather forcefully that large numbers of little governments are a concomitant of rural life. It suggests further that the downward trend in the number of units of local government is likely to continue, since reversal of the trend toward increasing urbanization appears quite improbable.

The Expectations of Rural Government

The forms of little government—rural county, small municipality, township, petty school district, and minor special district—are in harmony with the American heritage of agrarian democracy. If logic in structure and relationships and general satisfaction of consumer needs are passed over in favor of emphasis on government close to the people—why this, too, is in keeping with long tradition. Ours not to reason why: ours not to question the popular base of local government or the representativeness of its institutions, to wonder whether there is a viable relationship between a local unit and

the service it essays to perform, to doubt the soundness
of local administrative organization or the wisdom of
local leadership; ours but to embrace the proposition
that local government, and more especially rural local
government, is desirable and therefore in all important
respects good. "Local governments are to total government what basic tissues are to the human body. Without them, government would have no vitality."* Important contributions to our democratic life are expected, or assumed, of grass-roots government.

Among the positive virtues long presumed to inhere
in rural government is the easy intimacy which is
thought to flow from personal acquaintanceship. When
the chores of governance are discharged by friends and
neighbors, the citizen feels that he "belongs." He has
ready access to local officials; and if he cannot get
around to their place of business during the day, he
can chat things over with them on the doorstep in the
evening. Further, local problems are both more under-
standable and more manageable. Not only does the
citizen deal with public officers who are friends of
long acquaintance; both citizen and official deal with
local problems, with matters with which they are entirely familiar through personal contact. This means,
among other things, that the machinery and procedures
of government can be kept simple. There is no need
for checkers to check checkers, no occasion for multiple
signatures, no reason for copies in quintuplicate. Further still, those elected (or appointed) to public place
are well acquainted with local conditions; the problems
which require attention will be truly *local* in nature
for they will be identified and treated as such by the
friends and neighbors who occupy public office.

* *Local Government,* a report by the Advisory Committee on Local
Government to the Commission on Inter-Governmental Relations
(Washington: U. S. Government Printing Office, 1955), p. 9.

The votaries of rural life make much of grass-roots government as the schoolroom of democracy. De Tocqueville gave early statement to this doctrine in his observation that "the American . . . takes a lesson in the forms of government from governing. The great work of society is ever going on before his eyes and, as it were, under his hands." An official report published in 1955 echoes this view in somewhat more specific terms: "The counties, cities, towns, villages, and boroughs serve as training schools for the leaders of government and in the affairs of local government are tried those who aspire to State and National office."* Not only do leaders serve their apprenticeships in local affairs; citizens familiarize themselves with public issues through open discussion and through personal participation. They develop a "feel" for democratic government, a sense of what is right and what is wrong through the give-and-take of individual involvement. In the schoolroom of democracy, politics is direct, easygoing, and informal. There is no political machine in the sense in which the large cities know machines, if for no other reason than that the rewards of victory are not such as to make political striving worth while. There are, however, other reasons, found in the virtue of the people, the openness and forthrightness of public transactions, and the simplicity of governmental machinery.

A final positive advantage claimed for little government rests upon an administrative consideration. Many of the programs of government, even in some instances those closest to the people, are pursued under laws or regulations of larger governments—the state and sometimes even the federal government. The laws and rules interpreted and applied by rural officials are modified

* *Idem.*

in ways which make them both acceptable to the people
and applicable to the conditions of the local areas. Thus
is the uniformity of general need brought into harmony with the fact of diversity in local cultural, economic, and social patterns.

There is also a reverse side to this coin; for if rural
government is possessed of many positive virtues, it em-
bodies also a number of negative advantages. To illustrate, to the extent that a local unit administers its
own affairs, it avoids the threat of central, distant, and
impersonal control by an anonymous "foreign" government. It averts government by generalization in favor
of government by geographic specialization. Thus, further, it either circumvents or ameliorates the evils of
bureaucracy. It also escapes involvement in the big and
presumably bad politics of larger governments.

The expectations of rural government thus rest upon
two sets of propositions. The first emphasizes the ab-
solute advantages of little government, the second its
relative advantages as compared with big government.
Grass-roots government is held to be direct, personal,
intimate, informal, face-to-face; the entire atmosphere
makes for a spirit of democracy; the contacts of the
administrator are with the client or customer direct;
and there is a minimum of paperwork and of record-
keeping, for democracy is not a thing to be written
down but only to be experienced. The home rule
movement for cities and counties gives tangible evidence of the widespread conviction that local governments can attend to their own affairs more successfully
and with greater satisfaction than they can be attended
to from the state capitol. By contrast, big government
is held to represent the opposite of almost everything
that little government stands for; it is indirect, impersonal, anonymous, distant, formal; the contacts between
administrator and client-customer are long distance and

customarily are handled by mail, often by exchange of form communications; big democracy emphasizes procedures and is a stickler for observance of regulations; there administration is in essence paperwork, with the administrator often coming to regard the record as the end product of a given transaction and the prime object of his concern. Thus do the easy, comfortable ways of government at the grass roots give way to the worship of forms under the watchful guidance of a jealous bureaucracy. The contrast is a severe one, seeing that the American people must live the rest of their days with big government as well as little, but it is not more severe than the grass-roots rationale warrants.

The Physiology of Little Government

Here, then, is a complex structure for dealing with the public problems of rural America, and here are the interests which grass-roots government is expected to serve. It is in order now to examine the workings of rural government, not for its day-to-day operations but for its characteristic features. The purpose here is to describe, not to appraise. Criticism, even diagnosis, is forsworn for the present except as it may be inferred from a descriptive account.

Among the several characteristic features of little government is its part-time character. Of all the employees of municipalities of 5,000 inhabitants and less, only 37 per cent are full-time. This is suggestive of the nature of rural government, though it is necessary to add quickly that there are many thousands of local units which have no full-time employees at all. From the point of view of the employee, there are uncounted thousands of farmers, lawyers, mechanics, doctors, merchants, and housewives who devote one or two hours a day or one or two days a week (in some cases, five to ten days a year) to public employment. As an example, there is the Mayor of the small municipality (population 2,000) whose means of livelihood is his building materials business. Sought out at his shop (he rarely went to the one-room city hall), he chatted familiarly about municipal affairs. Presently the talk veered around to the Mayor's future plans, in particular reference to current street talk about a movement for the council-manager plan. "I won't run again," the Mayor said with finality, "but if they want a city manager, I'll take the job, and I won't charge 'em any $3,000, either." There are the three elected officials called listers (assessors) of the Vermont town, who work for only a few days each year except in the fourth year when real estate is re-assessed, when for a while they are quite busy. Secretaries, recorders, clerks, tax assessors, tax collectors, attorneys, engineers, treasurers, directors of recreation—here is an abbreviated list of the officers and employees who in rural government normally serve only part-time, when, indeed, they are found at all.

There is, of course, a way to make full-time work from these numerous part-time jobs, and that is by combining several kinds of duties under one office. The New England town clerk performs a great variety of chores, enough in a sizable town to warrant full-time employment. The clerk of a certain small southern municipality of record (population 1,800) serves as city clerk, treasurer, treasurer and purchasing agent for the water works board, tax collector, secretary to the city council, secretary to the mayor, clerk of the recorder's (mayor's) court, jailer, member of the volunteer fire department, member of the school board, member of the recreation board, city weigher, and notary public. On the side, by way of piecing out a living, he sells insurance and real estate, hires out as a public accountant, and buys and sells cotton. To complete his schedule, he teaches a Sunday School class and plays shortstop on the Lions' Club softball team. One is reminded of Pooh-Bah of *The Mikado,* who served as First Lord of the Treasury, Lord Chief Justice, Commander-in-Chief, Lord High Admiral, Master of the Buckhounds, Groom of the Back Stairs, Archbishop of Titipu, and Lord Mayor, both acting and elect. Here is a way to stop under-employment in its tracks!

A second feature of rural government is that it is almost wholly amateur, as indeed it must be in view of the foregoing. It is amateur in two senses. First, there are few of the tools of professional management now widely in use among the larger units; there is no regularized merit system, no budget system, no competitive purchasing, no double-entry accounting. To most rural administrators, these concepts remain in the realm of the far-away and the theoretical, for their equipment and procedures are rudimentary in the extreme. A small-town Mayor, hearing from a lecturer that the mayor's secretary should control the boss' telephone and appointment calendar, leaned over and whispered to the man in the next chair, "That's very interesting, but what do you do if you don't have a secretary?"

Little government is amateur in the further sense that its personnel is not professional. There is the clerk of a circuit court who by common consent knows nothing whatever about the duties of her office, but who manages to hold on because the local lawyers take turns at helping her with her work. There is the rural registrar who denied a Negro the right to vote because he could not "interrupt" the Constitution. In the same section, several registrars were found denying the right to vote to prospective voters (both Negro and white) because they could not interpret the Constitution, notwithstanding there was no such legal requirement. There is the case of the rural county which hired a retired railway express employee and gave him the title of "purchasing agent." After eight months in office, it was learned that the new person had participated in only two competitive purchase procedures. His salary as a part-time clerical person was $25 per month.

It is hardly necessary to emphasize that the part-time amateur government which is beginning to emerge is also quite casual in nature. A recent visitor to a rural county courthouse threaded his way up the steps through a group of six or eight men who were basking in the sunshine. His business carried him to the office of the tax collector, who, the sole clerk and attendant informed him, was out front. She fared forth to return presently with one of the men who had been sitting on the steps. When the visitor had finished his business with the tax collector, he inquired as to the county clerk. "Across the hall," said the official, nodding, "but he ain't there; he's out front." Then he stepped to the door of his office, aimed in the general direction of the front entrance, and called, "Hey, Ed, he wants you!" whereupon a second member of the group taking the sun pulled himself up and sauntered in. In another rural county, original county records were being copied at home by a housewife working part-time; when her employer's attention was called to the risk to his records through loss or damage, he required the typist to do her work in the office. In one of the smaller towns of Vermont, a representative of five successive generations of one family has served as town clerk, and the town's records have been kept in the clerk's family home for a century. A recent survey of town government in that state brought to light instances of official records kept on the backs of envelopes and on bits of scratch paper. Louis Brownlow tells a story of a local school board

meeting held in Charlottesville, Virginia, in the early
years of the last century. The board met on a street
corner and transacted its business without fanfare, and
also without reading of minutes, agenda, or other *Robert's Rules* items. The three members present were
Thomas Jefferson, James Madison, and James Monroe.

Local government in rural America is (or may be)
highly personal. A sheriff in a rural county some years
ago learned that two communist votes had been cast in
a local election. "I guess I broke every law there is
trying to find out who cast those ballots," he confided.
A visitor to a small municipality left his topcoat in
the office of the city clerk while the two went out to
lunch. Returning, he discovered that his coat had been
taken. The city clerk was chagrined, but not defeated.
"I'll just have the council appropriate money for a
new coat," he said. In New England, the town overseer
of the poor is expected to keep the poor of his town
from leaving and descending upon other towns; he is
also charged with the responsibility of protecting his
town against the poor seeking entrance from the outside. In Kansas, a farmer complained that Johnson grass
was spreading to his field from the neighboring county
road right-of-way, and ultimately was successful in per-
suading the county commissioners to declare that grass
a noxious weed, thus bringing it within the scope of
the public weed eradication program. Here, by the
way, is an excellent illustration of the way by which
a function long considered private comes to be taken
over by government. Here was no grasping bureaucracy
seeking new worlds to conquer, but only a farmer seeking to keep his field free of Johnson grass.

Rural local government also has its private (or pro-
prietary) aspects. A small-county judge complained that
"the new law requiring a medical examination before
a marriage license can be issued has cut my business

$25 a month." Rural county officials habitually refer
to the issuance of a license as a "sale." In one county,
the clerk each month computes what is owed to the
various state agencies for the licenses issued during the
month and the judge remits checks for these amounts,
transferring what is left to his personal account. (The
state examiners regularly find his accounts in good
order.) A rural legislator, in explanation of a proposed
local bill, said, "Last session I raised my probate judge
to $3,600 and my commissioners to $1,500, but their
morale hasn't been too good so I'm giving them another
little raise now."

There are occasions when grass-roots government
takes on the character of an eleemosynary enterprise.
A clerk is kept on because, though not satisfactory, she
"needs the job." Another is retained because "he's
crippled and can't do anything else." Many local office-holders run their own private systems of relief. One
rural county judge, explaining his periodic disappear-
ances into the vault room with constituents, observed
that people requested him to step into the vault when
they wanted to ask for help. "It costs me a couple of
dollars every time I go into the vault," he said. A rural
state legislature some years ago refused to switch to
typewriters for enrolling bills because some of the copy-
ists who wrote well enough by hand were not able to
type. A certain grass-roots county judge will not allow
a hard-pressed constituent to become delinquent for
want of payment of a license fee. As a consequence, he
has advanced some $4,000 in petty personal loans over
the course of the last several years.

In many respects rural government is anachronistic,
being closely wedded (as is all government, indeed) to
the past. The New England towns, the oldest of local
governments in America, generally have eliminated the
culler of hoop poles, staves, and headings, in recognition

of the passing of the barrel; and the rural schools have abolished the post of wood inspector, which was necessary in other days to ensure that each patron contributed his share to the winter's wood supply. In Vermont, however, each town still must appoint three fence viewers, who are charged to see that fences are kept in order and in the proper location. A tree warden likewise must be appointed to keep the public shade trees in good condition. The organization of grass-roots government is almost wholly outmoded, but that is a subject not appropriate for examination here.

Rural local government, for all its seeming simplicity, can become quite complicated. The average citizen lives within and has at least some dealings with not less than four units of government: the nation, the state, the county, and the municipality. He frequently finds himself resident within three or four units in addition—township, school district, soil conservation district, and so on. The result is that residence within seven or eight overlying units is not uncommon. These units normally were established with little or no thought for the convenience of the citizen, who often is not able to differentiate one government or one program from the other.

Little government, being personal, intimate, and informal, is supposed by some to be free of politics. In simple truth, no concept concerning local government has less merit. The image of politics as an evil art practiced somewhere else by somebody else is, of course, quite unrealistic; for politics is found wherever people debate issues of public import. Grass-roots politics frequently involves little of public policy; on the contrary, it may be largely of a personal character, and it may indeed be cast in terms of personal loyalty rather than in those usually held appropriate to the public arena. For all that the citizen, and more particularly the minor

office-holder or employee, will discover quickly in
what direction the imperatives lie, and he will experience prompt and sure retribution if he does not hew
to the established line. A rural county commissioner
elected on a "reform" platform found the ground cut
from under him in one deft move when the county
board abolished the district system and brought the
construction and maintenance of county roads under
the direct supervision of the board. Here was as effective and as ruthless a political move as ever was en-
gineered by a big city boss.

Last among the features of rural government to be
examined here is the basic nature of the process of
governance at the grass roots. The student of public
affairs distinguishes broadly between government, politics, and administration; but in little government these
distinctions are not valid, or if valid in principle, are
not overly useful in practice. The smaller the unit or
area is, the closer the government is to the grass roots,
the less meaningful is the distinction between politics,
government, and administration; the larger the unit
or area, the sharper the distinction. Grass-roots government is therefore pre-eminently the domain of the
generalist, big government that of the specialist. Big
government needs the generalist, of course, and it is,
indeed, one of the prime problems of public administration to develop managers with a general sense of
government and administration. Little government by
contrast has generalists in plenty; for there the lines
separating politics from government and both from
administration blur and grow dim, with the result that
nothing more than a general impression of government
remains. The differentiations in process common in
big government are hardly known at the grass roots.

Rural local government, then, is different; it is so
decidedly different from the "local government" of

the textbooks as to be hardly recognizable from the generalizations found there. There is nothing whatever, beyond a legal fiction, in common between, say, Cleveland, Ohio, and Auburn, West Virginia. The action of the Mayor of a Kentucky village in adjourning a council meeting (with apologies to the visitor present) at 4:00 o'clock so that the council members could get home to do their milking before dark would prove utterly incomprehensible to the mayor and council members of any of the larger cities. Yet this incident did occur, and many others like it occur every day in the little governments of America. This is government at the grass roots. It is not important in terms of functions performed, personnel employed, or money spent, but it does stand as the guardian of the American tradition of rural democracy.

iii Little Government: Appraisal

IN THIS ESSAY it is proposed to evaluate rural government in terms of structure, administration, and the practice of democracy. Due to the long-standing habit, especially among those predisposed toward local government, of confusing grass-roots government with local democracy, and even of identifying the one with the other, it is necessary to emphasize that it is *rural government* which is under appraisal. There is a distinct tendency to construe a criticism of local government as an attack on democracy, and so by a not unnatural inversion to defend democracy in terms of the prevailing structure and practice of local government. This habit of thought, which stems direct from the tenets of Jeffersonian agrarianism, straitjackets democracy in a mold which was set a century and a half ago, and precludes discussion of that subject as a live and vital thing.

It is the thesis here that democracy and rural local government not only can be analyzed independently but that they are indeed completely separate things. Democracy is to be weighed in terms appropriate to a particular day or age. So is rural government, if it is to be viewed realistically. To the extent that grass-roots government has adapted itself to changing social, economic, and political requirements, it has, it may be supposed, equipped itself to serve positively the cause of democracy; but to the extent that it has resisted adaptation to mid-twentieth century needs, it may well have become anti-democratic in content and effect. In any event, the champions of grass-roots government must not be allowed to identify themselves as being *ipso facto* the defenders of democracy, and the only true defenders. Such champions, in fact, often will be discovered on examination to be defenders of the *status quo*. The marriage between little government and democracy thus becomes a device, though sometimes an unconscious one, by which the rural "fortress of anachronistic privileges" is defended in terms of principles dear to the nation. The principles of democracy are indeed traditional and enduring, but their invocation in defense of a particular political institution is a dangerous thing.

Apart from the unwarranted employment of democracy in defense of rural government, there is credible authority for the proposition that democracy and local government are mutually antagonistic. De Tocqueville was among those who early maintained that the government in a democratic nation ". . . must be more uniform, more centralized, more extensive, more searching, and more efficient than in other countries." A present-day student developed this thesis in a recent article, maintaining that democracy is by definition broad in view, equalitarian, majoritarian, unitarian; it emphasizes the social whole, avoiding the atomization which necessarily follows the interposition of any intermediary between the state and the individual. Local government, on the other hand, is a phenomenon of differentiation and individualization; it represents and seeks to strengthen separate social groups enjoying a measure of autonomy which sometimes becomes virtual independence. Democracy and local government are therefore in an important sense antithetical; ". . . the incompatibility of democratic principle with the practice of decentralization is a phenomenon so evident that it may be considered as a kind of sociological law."*

It is not necessary to accept this view in order to justify question of the logic by which rural government is equated with democracy. One may stop far short of the position assumed by Langrod and still conclude that the arrogation of all democratic virtues by the champions of grass-roots government is presumptuous and indefensible. The focus of the present discussion is on rural government, not on democracy. If the practice of rural government emerges somewhat the worse from this analysis, as almost inevitably it must, it will be well always to remember where the emphasis lies.

The Institutions of Little Government

The earlier table portraying the units of government in the United States afforded a general view of the superstructure of local government. It revealed that, in 1952, there were 116,743 units of government in existence, all but 49 of them local units. The accompanying table makes possible a somewhat more detailed analysis of the number and kind of local units within a restricted area. As it indicates, there are (or were in 1952) sixteen counties each having 200 or more units of local government. Only five of these counties have more than 150,000 people, and the largest of the remaining eleven has only a few more than 80,000. The table confirms the earlier impression that there is a direct correlation between number of local governments and rurality.

Four of the counties listed have populations of less than 25,000 each, and two have fewer than 15,000 people. One of the latter (Holt, Nebraska) ranks tenth in total number of units of local government, sixth

---

* Georges Langrod, "Local Government and Democracy," *Public Administration*, Vol. XXXI (Spring, 1953), 25-34.

DISTRIBUTION OF LOCAL GOVERNMENTAL UNITS IN SIXTEEN COUNTIES
HAVING 200 OR MORE UNITS EACH, 1952

County	State	Number of Local Governments	Municipalities	Townships	School Districts	Special Districts	Population (1950)
Cook	Illinois	422	99	30	164	128	4,508,792
Otter Tail	Minnesota	334	20	62	249	2	51,320
Dane	Wisconsin	292	24	35	226	6	169,357
Custer	Nebraska	276	11	30	230	4	19,170
Stearns	Minnesota	271	29	37	203	1	70,681
Grant	Wisconsin	255	19	33	202	—	41,460
Allegheny	Pennsylvania	247	80	47	116	3	1,515,237
Polk	Minnesota	237	15	59	160	2	35,900
Suffolk	New York	233	27	10	114	81	276,129
Holt	Nebraska	226	8	36	179	2	14,859
Marathon	Wisconsin	218	14	42	161	—	80,337
Fillmore	Minnesota	214	14	23	174	2	24,465
Kent	Michigan	214	10	24	177	2	288,292
Dodge	Wisconsin	205	15	24	164	1	57,611
Fond du Lac	Wisconsin	204	10	21	165	7	67,829
Knox	Nebraska	201	10	30	150	10	14,820
Total		4,049	405	543	2,834	251	7,236,259
Percentage Distribution		100.0	10.0	13.4	70.0	6.2	(Counties, 0.4)

(among those listed) in number of townships, and sixth in number of school districts. The smallest county ranks third in number of special districts. In number of townships, rural counties rank first and second. Of the five counties having more than 200 school districts each, four are rural. The county with the greatest number of school districts is a rural county, while at the other extreme the two lowest counties in number of school districts are metropolitan counties.

Over-all, the table reveals that 0.5 per cent of the total number of counties have 3.4 per cent of the units of local government. If the five counties having populations of 150,000 each are eliminated, the eleven rural counties remaining, 0.36 per cent of the total number possessing 0.32 per cent of the nation's population, have 2.3 per cent of the units of local government. These eleven rural counties are therefore "over-represented," so to speak, more than six times in the matter of prevalence of local units.

Certain conclusions may be generalized from the table. First, either some counties are greatly over-organized, in terms of need for local governmental units, or many are grossly under-organized. It is wholly likely that the advantage lies with the first alternative. Second, excessive proliferation of little government is more characteristic of rural areas than of urban, though not limited to one or the other. Third, the states having the largest numbers of units of local government are concentrated in the Midwest; all but two of the sixteen counties listed are located in that region, and twelve of them are situated in Minnesota, Nebraska, and Wisconsin. The table does not show this, but the eight leading states, in terms of number of local governments, lie in the Midwest, with Minnesota at the head of the list and Nebraska second. Of the eight states having an average number of 75 or more governmental

units per county, six are midwestern, with Minnesota
again in the lead with an average of 104 units per
county and Wisconsin second with 102. North Dakota,
South Dakota, Nebraska, Kansas, Minnesota, Iowa, Missouri, Wisconsin, Illinois, and Michigan, ten states, contain 58 per cent of all the units of government in the
country. Their leadership in this questionable field is
to be attributed largely to the concentration of the
township and (more especially) the school district in
the Middle West: 60 per cent of all townships are found
in the states listed, 67 per cent of all school districts.*
These ten midwestern states contain well over four-
fifths of all non-operating school districts in the country, and more than half of all one-teacher schools.

The full import of the fragmentation of government
locally begins to appear when it is remembered that
federal, state, and local governments operate simultaneously in a given area. Not only are there overlying
local units created for special purposes and operating
in substantial independence; there are state agents and
agencies, and federal representatives as well, active
locally in related but substantially independent program fields. Thus the local council on intergovernmental relations for Blue Earth County (1940 population, 35,000), Minnesota, found that there were 155
local units of government in the county, including,
besides the county itself, 23 townships, two cities, seven
villages, and 122 school districts. In addition, the council discovered that 105 state agencies were in operation
in the county and that 38 federal agencies likewise had
interests there. Here, then, were almost 300 units and

---

* Further to confuse the image of local government, let it be noted
there there are uncounted thousands of administrative and other
special-purpose districts which do not qualify as units of government
and so are not taken into account in this discussion.

48   GRASS ROOTS

agencies of government doing business either full-time
or some-time in one small county.

Henry County (1940 population, 43,000), Indiana,
fared even worse numerically: there cities, villages,
townships, school districts, and county to the number
of 110 units were joined by 111 state and 106 federal
agencies, for a total of 327 units and agencies of government in business in the county. The Henry County
Council found that ". . . due to unrelated development
of governments, overlapping exists within and between
all levels of government."* The council reported serious
intergovernmental friction arising from excessive and
overly-restrictive regulations; over-emphasis on uniformity; lack of knowledge of local conditions and lack of appreciation of local needs by "outside administrators";
performance of the same or similar services by different
agencies, with resultant confusion, irritation, expense,
and rivalry; failure on the part of officials adequately
to explain, and on the part of citizens to understand,
new services, particularly departures involving major
changes in practice; failure of the merit system to operate satisfactorily because of excessive rigidity; and a
disposition on the part of local officials to make undue
concessions in the face of "demonstrations of strength"
by state and (more especially) federal officials. The bill
of particulars is significant not only for the problem
areas cited, but also for the smoldering resentment
against "outside interference" implicit in its tone.

The net result of this governmental wilderness for
the public employees themselves is one of confusion,
or would be if they were concerned with the rationalization of government; for the citizen, it is one of complete and utter dismay. He does not know what government is represented by an official with whom he

* Council of Intergovernmental Relations, *Grass Roots: A Report
and Evaluation* (Washington, 1947), pp. 28-29.

has dealings; he does not know where his tax money goes, or what services it purchases; he does not understand the jurisdictional differences which divide among minute cells the many employees who appear to him to be generally bent on the same business. His despair of understanding takes the form of a defensiveness against government and all its works; and since he is acquainted, at least by hearsay, with the local officials, he turns his resentment on a government so large and so distant as to seem anonymous. "The Government" comes to mean the government in Washington, its millions and its minions, its processes and its papers and their copies in quintuplicate, and above all its bureaucracy. In local parlance, all federal employees are bureaucrats, an exception being made, of course, in the case of the Soil Conservation Service employee who lives next door; while no state or local official is ever so stigmatized. Government and governors thus emerge in popular fancy as a huge conspiracy, in some part at least because government even locally seems so aimless, shapeless, and detached.

Contemplation of the machinery of government leads to speculation on the role of ritual in modern society. Anthropologists have observed that practices regarded with veneration by one society are viewed with abhorrence by another, that matters of seemingly little import sometimes are defended tooth and nail while concerns of grave moment are left unattended or to chance —that, in short, what is held to be important and what not varies greatly and without apparent reason from society to society. The enduring fact is the continuing observance of ritual or custom long after the occasion which gave it birth has passed. It is so in matters of governance, even within the limits of one country. In the United States there is a common (or it may be an uncommon) language, there is an inspiring national

history covering now almost two centuries, there are
widely held aspirations and ideals and a native devotion
to democracy. Yet one state maintains a vast superstructure of local government while another equally
populous makes out with one-tenth as much, one state
harbors 6,000 school districts while another has none,
one state preserves a thousand townships while another
abolishes all such units—and all in the name of the twin
gods of efficiency and democracy. Never was there a
better illustration of the gulf between "inspirational
statements of tribal objectives and the performance
which they symbolize." The paraphernalia of little government manifestly represents rural America's ongoing
commitment to the concepts of another day.

Rural Government and Administration

The folklore of agrarian America insists not only
that the country provides the best of all possible ways
of life, but that the little governments which have come
into being to serve rural needs are at once administratively more efficient and more democratic than any
other. Lord Bryce was moved to comment thus on this
state of mind: "Americans often reply to the criticisms
which Europeans pass on the faults of their State legislatures and the shortcomings of Congress by pointing
to the healthy efficiency of their rural administration,
which enables them to bear with composure the defects
of the higher organs of government. . . ." The assumptions regarding the effectiveness of grass-roots government are worthy of analysis. In the examination which
follows, it is well to remember that the subject under
appraisal is *little* government, not local government.

In evaluating a unit of government in terms of its
administrative adequacy, a number of basic considerations must be kept in mind. The first concerns the
functions to be performed, which must be sufficient

in number, variety, and significance to challenge the interest of both the public servant and the citizen. If the services required are picayune, if it is a matter of little importance whether or not they get done, if the business of government is nothing more than busy-work, the unit may be suspected of being without justification in terms of function. Second, the *population* to be served is of basic importance. If the residents within a unit are so few as to provide an inadequate consumer base, or to allow of no choice in filling the offices of government, the unit obviously is too small in terms of people.

Third, *geographical adequacy* is always an important factor. The boundaries of a unit of government should be defined in terms of both the functions to be performed and the population to be served, and should take into account such considerations as topography and distance. The latter criterion changes continuously in response to steady improvements in communication and transportation, so that standards of geographical layout which were sound fifty years ago have little current application, and units which were of convenient size then are now entirely too small. Fourth, *fiscal adequacy* is a fundamental factor in determining the administrative soundness of a unit of government. Rural government remains dependent very largely upon the general property tax, which means that a local unit must have available a sufficient tax base, in terms of real and personal property, to produce the revenue required to run its government. Property values therefore provide a standard for judging the administrative potential of a unit from which, given the existing tax structure, there is no effective appeal.

Fifth, the opportunity for the introduction of *technical competence* into the government must be taken into account. Such competence may concern fiscal affairs: budget officers, accountants, and purchasing agents are technicians. It may also concern such professional fields as law, engineering, and medicine. If a unit of government is not large enough, in terms of variety of functions to be performed, size of population, and fiscal resources, to permit a measure of administrative specialization, then its right to continued existence deserves to be challenged. Another aspect of the same problem has to do with the professional attitude which is introduced into the local employee group along with personnel of special training, experience, and competence. Finally, the administration of rural affairs is likely to be more effective if public issues can be approached from the *general rather than the special* or piecemeal point of view. This means that the cause of administration is best served if there is only one unit of local government in a given area, and it charged with all authority and responsibility necessary for the conduct of local affairs.

In terms of the six criteria which have been suggested, how much of the machinery of rural government qualifies as potentially sound administratively? Let us pass the units of grass-roots government in review: 24 per cent of all counties have less than 10,000 people each; 56 per cent of all municipalities have populations of less than 1,000, 86 per cent have fewer than 5,000; 64 per cent of the townships have less than 1,000 people each, 86 per cent have less than 2,500; there are more than 47,000 one-teacher schools, and 66 per cent of all school districts enroll fewer than fifty pupils each; and 75 per cent of the special districts are of small consequence by any comparative standards. These figures hint at the administrative poverty of grass-roots government in the United States. They suggest that little government may be neither efficient nor economical by any of the criteria listed above.

The per capita costs of county government have been found to diminish sharply with increasing population to 30,000, and thereafter to level off. If the minimum desirable size for counties were fixed at 30,000 population, some 2,000 counties, or 65 per cent of the total number, would be eliminated. Among those which would suffer extinction would be all grass-roots counties. If one of the principal functions of rural administration, road building and maintenance, were taken over by the counties, as has been suggested, virtually all townships could be eliminated as units of substantive government. As regards a second primary function of rural government, school administration, the fixing of a minimum school population of 1,500 pupils per district, as has been responsibly recommended, would result in the abolition of 96.5 per cent of the present school districts. A committee of the National Association of Assessing Officers, reporting some years ago on assessment organization and personnel, recommended that minimum standards of local tax assessment districts be fixed at 10,000 population and $10 million assessed valuation.* The committee went on to say, however, that very few assessment districts met these quite modest standards: 88 per cent of all (primary) local assessment districts had populations of less than 5,000. The committee also recommended a minimum annual appropriation of $5,000 to cover the cost of property assessment in a district. Almost none of the local assessment districts enjoyed such generous support; among the units of rural local government, indeed, there are large numbers whose annual budgets do not total $5,000 for all purposes.

Among the services which the grass-roots units of general government—the 762 counties of less than

* National Association of Assessing Officers, *Assessment Organization and Personnel* (Chicago, 1941), p. 54.

10,000 and the 9,467 municipalities of less than 1,000 inhabitants—find it impossible to provide are police and fire protection, public health, and public welfare. It is not meant to imply that no small government maintains any of these services: some do, of course, and some on a reasonably satisfactory basis. The great majority, however, find all excepting the most rudimentary services, and these performed in quite elementary fashion, beyond their resources. Hansen and Perloff cite conclusive evidence that "economic resources rather than need determine the level of service . . ." in the smaller and poorer units.*

The outlook for rural government is no brighter with respect to administrative organization and procedure. Sound fiscal administration is beyond the reach of the minor units. The part-time, amateur character of the rural functionary militates against development of a professional public service. So does the method of compensation, which would be totally inadequate if competent service were demanded or expected. Nor is the method of selection calculated to ensure choice of competent personnel. Local officers and employees, including specifically most of the chief administrative officials of the county, are chosen by popular vote, which virtually all students agree is not the best way to fill a position whose duties require technical competence. The system by which the duties and responsibilities of office are divided, both through the fragmentation of functions within a unit and through duplication with overlying areas, likewise is destructive of the environment in which a competent and professionally motivated public service might thrive. Another aspect of the same problem is found in the lack of in-

* Alvin H. Hansen and Harvey S. Perloff, *State and Local Finance in the National Economy* (New York: W. W. Norton & Company, 1944), p. 23.

tegration among the various segments of the administrative organization. In short, there is regrettably little of professional spirit or conduct in the affairs of grass-roots government. The administrative structure is ill-organized and poorly manned, while the procedures and systems of public management are largely alien to the rural scene.

What is required more than any other one thing for the administrative rehabilitation of rural government is a system which will command the confidence and respect of the citizen. A government which has no important services to perform, or which does not have resources adequate to its needs, or which is so inconsequential that it must content itself with part-time and amateur service, or which is satisfied to drift along an administrative channel marked out a century ago and not changed since, or which approaches the public's problems timidly and half-heartedly, or which shares responsibilities with a dozen or a hundred other units and agencies—such a government will not enjoy because it will not have earned the confidence of the people. The first and most important lesson to be learned about grass-roots democracy is that local government, like government at other levels, must be strong, energetic, and well supported if it is to discharge with satisfaction the duties which modern conditions impose upon it. Grass-roots government unhappily does not now answer that description, notwithstanding the pervasive mythology to the contrary.

Rural Government and Democracy

It appears from the foregoing that very large numbers of local governments are too small and weak to operate efficiently in administrative terms. It is appropriate to inquire whether these same units may not also be too small to be effectively democratic. What

could the towns of Glastenbury (population seven) and
Somerset (population twenty), Vermont, do that would
be of any real significance? Each was dominated by
one family, and each was entitled to its representative
in the state legislative body. The representative of one
failed to put in an appearance for the whole of a
legislative session; the representative of the other, however, was on hand every meeting day to protect his
family's right to representation—and to the taxes paid
(nominally to the town, but actually to the family) by
the power company. Both of these towns were disestab-
lished by the General Assembly twenty years ago, but
not until long after they (and others like them) had
brought the honorable tradition of town government
in New England to disrepute. One of the things most
needed to permit a reasoned judgment of the grass-roots
practice of democracy is an examination of the folklore
enveloping the subject.

It will prove useful to begin with an analysis of the
tacit (sometimes the explicit) assumption of the devotees of agrarian democracy that Lilliputian government is more democratic *per se* than big government.
The argument runs thus: government to be democratic
must be close to the people; little government is close
to the people, and the smaller it is the closer it is; therefore the smaller the units of government and the larger
their number the greater the degree of democracy. A
companion line holds that little government tends to
be more democratic than big government because it
lacks the incentive, the resources, and the power to be
otherwise; it is democratic, so to speak, by default.

A 1955 Census publication *(State Distribution of
Public Employment in 1954)* provides an interesting
basis for speculation on this subject. It reads in part:

> The range for State governments (full-time equivalent)
> in October 1954 was from 45 [employees] per 10,000

[inhabitants] for Illinois up to 177 per 10,000 for North Carolina. The range for local government employment was from 58 per 10,000 in North Carolina up to 265 per 10,000 in New York State.

In 1952 North Carolina had 106 special districts, Illinois 1,546, New York 968; North Carolina had no school districts, while Illinois had 3,484 and New York 2,915; North Carolina had no township governments, Illinois had 1,433 and New York 932. The conclusion to be drawn from these figures, within the framework of traditional thinking about rural government, is clear: North Carolina's government is less close to the people and therefore is less democratic than that of either Illinois or New York.

One who looks beneath the surface will reject this proposition both as being too pat and as resting upon inadequate evidence. It is true that in relation to population North Carolina has the largest number of state employees and the smallest number of local employees of any state in the union. This is attributable largely to the fact that in North Carolina the state government has assumed primary responsibility for a number of important functions traditionally left largely to the localities, among them public school administration and road construction and maintenance. With the passing of administrative responsibility from the local units (principally the counties) to the state has gone a shift in the incidence of public employment, though so far as the testimony at hand reveals without adverse effect on the practice of democracy in the state. It is also true that North Carolina has comparatively few units of government (608 as compared with Illinois' 7,723 and New York's 5,483). This fact, however, will hardly support the generalization that government in that state is less democratic than elsewhere—than in Illinois or New York, specifically. On the contrary, students of local government would maintain that North Carolina has taken a significant step along the path leading to local democracy by moving to clear away the undergrowth to make government visible to the citizen.

It must be concluded that smallness in size and multiplicity in number of rural governments provide neither a guarantee of the existence of nor a standard for measuring the effectiveness of local democracy. There are other and more meaningful criteria, among them the nature of popular participation, the representativeness of policy-making bodies, and the kind and efficacy of the control exercised over administrative officials. The relationship between the degree of democracy and the complexity of local governmental machinery is much more likely to be inverse than direct.

Second among the hallowed articles of faith is the tradition that the local community serves as the "schoolroom for democracy."* As a writer in a recent issue of the *National Municipal Review* put it, "The value of democracy is not open to question in this discussion. Assuming its virtue, there is little doubt that the most effective training ground for democracy lies in the field of local self-government." Here is the doctrine, naked and unadorned. It is worthy of analysis.

The author makes two basic assumptions. The first, that democracy is virtuous, few will wish to challenge; but the second, concerning the effectiveness of local self-government as a training ground for democracy, may be open to question. The assumption is that the citizen learns about democracy from participation in the affairs of local government. But what does he learn and how does he learn it? What is the curriculum offered? Who are the faculty? What are the teaching and

* The Little Green Schoolhouse, shall we call it, in succession to the Little Red Schoolhouse.

learning materials? To answer some of these questions, let it be noted that the citizen learns only about local affairs—that is, provincial and parochial affairs, that his teachers are small-time politicians and part-time functionaries, and that the courses of study are village pump politics and strictly amateur administration. The value of this kind of knowledge imparted in this fashion to the students of democracy is doubtful. The citizen so schooled in local government may develop a keen sense for sectional and special interests, but except by accident he will not graduate with a perceptive grasp of government in any broad or meaningful sense. Further, he is more than likely to emerge with a permanent bias against big government, and particularly against the federal government of the United States. The average grass-roots government as a schoolroom for democracy may be compared with the one-room public school, which is assailed on every hand by professional educators and which is sharply on the decline.

An important aspect of the "training ground" argument is found in the notion that persons trained in the rural arena go on to achieve renown on larger stages and before greater audiences. This assumption may be valid up to a point: it may well be that large numbers of state legislators gain their initial experience in public life from local office. Of the 31 state governors listed in *Who's Who* in 1954, however, only eleven confessed to previous local experience. Two-thirds therefore came to the gubernatorial office through other than local channels. Of the 96 United States senators in 1955, more than two-thirds (67) reported no experience in local government. Among the members of the House of Representatives, 71 per cent had had no experience as local office-holders. These figures do not dispose of the onward-and-upward argument, but they do suggest that the assumption on which the point rests deserves to be questioned. Grass-roots government as the Little Green Schoolhouse of democracy is another aspect of the agrarian mythology which requires re-examination.

Yet another phase of the myth concerns citizen participation in local affairs, both as candidate for public office and as voter. It appears to be generally assumed that non-participation poses no problem at the grass roots. A spokesman of the United States Department of Agriculture recently opined that "if all farmers could be members of a county land-use planning committee, planning would be entirely democratic as it is in some New England town meetings." In some town meetings maybe, but not in all, and perhaps in simple fact not in many. The New England town has played a prominent role in song and story for more than three centuries as America's chief exemplar of local democracy. Yet even in colonial times some of the towns found cause to question the presumed warmth of local patriotism. Boston, as a single example, was driven to levy a fine of ten pounds on any person who without good cause refused, having been elected, to serve as constable. In latter days, the problem of non-participation in town affairs has in many instances been acute. A credible reporter describes a town meeting which, with 700 adult citizens qualified to take part, was attended by 110 citizens who came and stayed most of the day. That is a participation figure of 15.7 per cent. An additional ninety citizens dropped by during the day to cast a vote on this or that issue and, having voted, went away. If these ninety are added to the original 110, total participation comes to 29 per cent; but were the ninety casual droppers-by participants in town affairs in any real sense? They were instead special pleaders who came in to vote on a single issue; their concern was a particular, fragmental one, and it may be argued with some logic that the cause of town government would have been better served and a consensus of citizen opinion more accurately recorded had these ninety remained at home with their special interests and left the decisions to those who came and stayed through the day.*

It would, of course, be erroneous to suppose that the problem of non-participation is a sectional one. An article in the *New York Times Magazine* some time ago carried the telling title, "Nobody Wants to be Town Clerk." "The people don't seem to understand the problems of town government," the author said of his Ohio town of 3,500 inhabitants. "Ninety-five per cent of the people don't even know who is on the Town Council. All official meetings are open to the public, but they seldom come to see what's going on." It is invidious to cite a particular illustration, for the reason that citizen non-participation is an almost universal phenomenon. Note was made earlier of the fact that farmer participation in the various local committees sponsored by the United States Department of Agriculture fell off sharply after the novelty of the committee system wore off. The apathy of the voter is widespread, and is alleviated only where an occasional scandal finds its way into the campaign or a flamboyant individual emerges as a candidate.

This does not mean that the attempted practice of democracy should be abandoned; it does not necessarily mean, indeed, that democracy does not exist even in the localities where citizen non-participation is most pronounced. A recent article in *Harper's Magazine* bore

* Andrew Nuquist, *Town Government*. Professor Nuquist, of the Department of Political Science of the University of Vermont, wrote a series of newspaper articles on town government in Vermont for the *Rutland Herald* beginning in October 1946 and running to midyear 1948. This citation is to a clipping file of those articles, which constitute the most perceptive examination of town government that has come to my attention.

the provocative title, "Let's Not Get Out The Vote."
The burden of its argument was that the citizen is not
duty-bound to vote, but that he is obligated to acquaint
himself with the candidates and the issues if he does
vote. Voter action or inaction is only one of the several
criteria appropriate to an evaluation of the workings
of democracy. For present purposes, however, attention
is centered on the fact that there is a marked lack of
citizen enthusiasm for voting at the grass-roots level.
The Little Green Schoolhouse is badly in need of a
truant officer.

Another cause for concern over democracy as it is
practiced in rural government arises from the representative system, and on two principal counts. First,
the legislative bodies are not representative; and second,
the procedures are neither democratic themselves nor
productive of democratic results. As to the first, most
legislative bodies, local and otherwise, consist of representatives elected by districts. This is true, for example,
of the typical rural county court (or board of commissioners or supervisors). In the states of the Middle
West the township is the election district; in the South
it is the precinct, or "beat." Everywhere, however, the
result is the same: district-sized men are elected to the
county governing body, with the consequence that a
"county legislature" prevails. This means that county
problems are viewed through myopic local eyes. It
means, for example, that bridges must be scattered
about the county in accordance with the residence of
the commissioners; it means that roads are parceled
out the same way; it means that a commissioner will
seize "his" road machinery with a firm grasp and refuse
to allow it to be used outside his own district. It means
finally, and of course most importantly, that the interests of the county are lost in those of the individual
election districts.

Other illustrations of faulty representative bodies can be found both below and above the county: the state legislature is a prime example of an important body normally dominated by district-minded members. The election districts vary greatly in size: in 1940 the ten smallest towns in Vermont, with a combined population of 857 persons, had ten representatives in the General Assembly; so had the ten largest towns and cities, with a total population of 116,811. A particularly vicious aspect of this unrepresentative system is found in the fact that election districts are almost never modified to take account of changes in population. The consequence is very great over-representation for the rural areas and equally marked under-representation for the cities. Georgia's notorious county-unit system is deliberately designed to assure to the rural districts perpetual control of that state's government. The rural-urban inequity is more striking in the case of the state legislature than in that of local representative bodies, but is by no means without example in grass-roots government.

Yet another aspect of the representative system which is worthy of note concerns the procedures employed in the legislatures. In South Carolina, to cite a single example, the state legislature is dominated by the various county delegations, as it is, indeed, in most states where the county is an important unit. In South Carolina, however, the hold of the counties on their representatives and of the county delegations in turn on the legislature appears to be particularly strong. As evidence, it may be noted that most of the measures passed by the legislature are local in import: of all bills passed over a period of 24 years recently ended, 83.9 per cent were local measures. Friday is the day set aside during a legislative session for consideration of local and uncontested matters. The question of a quorum by general agreement is never raised on that day, and a mere handful in each house proceeds to enact local measures. According to a recent count of a number of Friday meetings, the median meeting time for the House was six minutes. The Senate normally met for somewhat longer, though there was no effort in either house to give local bills any real consideration. They were passed by courtesy at the request of local delegations. Among the measures proposed by the 46 county delegations are the annual supply bills, one for each county. These bills are drafted by the delegations after local hearings and are passed as a matter of routine action by the legislature, almost always without question.

How democratic is a government whose legislative body is palpably unrepresentative in any real sense and whose practice is deliberately designed to serve the desires of ward and district delegates? Such a body is in fact more a congress of ambassadors than a legislative assembly. The system operates on the unspoken premise that what the five (or 25) county commissioners desire individually will add up to what is best for the county as a whole, that the 46 particularistic programs of the several county delegations in the aggregate will constitute a sound general legislative program for the state. It is not clear where responsibility for the welfare of the county or the state as a whole lies under this theory of representative government, but clearly it does not reside in any real sense in the representative body.

Concerning politics at the grass roots, it must be emphasized that political activities are in no wise the exclusive preserve of big government. In popular fancy the ultimate in politics is found in the manipulation of "the machine" by "the boss." The very concepts suggest the local character of machine politics. It is difficult to imagine the existence of either a national political machine or a national boss; statewide machines and bosses, indeed, have been rare phenomena. The natal place of party is the locality, where political organizations find a hospitable environment and where the phrase grass roots, in respect of politics, has tangible meaning. The notorious organizations in the past have been typically the big city (and county) machines, their managers the "bosses" of the muckrakers and their followers. Not less than three times in the last five years have the newspapers characterized a particular politician (a different one in each instance) as "the last of the big city bosses." The implication is clear that the supply of old-line urban machine politicians is running low.

Not so the supply of rural bosses, who continue in full production—and often in full command of tightly organized, highly disciplined machines. There must be, and there must always have been, a hundred nameless grass-roots bosses for every big city boss who found his way into the headlines. The case of the judge of a small southern county (1950 population somewhat more than 20,000) is instructive. That official, who had held a variety of local offices over a period of years and had served as county judge for twelve years at the time these facts were recorded, was complete and unquestioned arbiter of local affairs. He arranged candidacies for county offices, supervised elections to the end that there should be no recorded defections, referred patronizingly (but accurately) to "his" tax collector and "his" commissioners' court, operated his own personal system of poor relief, and so conducted the business of the county and the affairs of the local Democratic Party that they were virtually indistinguishable. So great was the faith of his associates in his leadership that there had not been a single dissenting vote on a matter brought before the commissioners' court in the

twelve years of his tenure as county judge. "In every
village," Sir Robert Peel once foretold, "there will arise
some miscreant, to establish the most grinding tyranny
by calling himself the people." This is a harsh prophecy,
and one hardly confirmed by our example; but it sounds
a warning not to be ignored. Grass-roots governments
have their machines and their bosses, too. And to para-
phrase a Chinese proverb, a small black spot is not less
black than a large black spot.

Machines and bosses apart, rural government is per-
meated by politics. One of the Public Administration
cases relates the story of a county agricultural conservation program committee which crossed swords with
an influential rancher on the question of the latter's
compliance or non-compliance with a ranch management plan previously approved by the committee. The
local contest ended in a draw, and the rancher's neighbors of the county committee were glad enough to buck
the case up to the state committee for final decision.*
In the *Rutland Herald* (Vermont) of November 10,
1946, the writer of a letter to the editor made some
remarks on the subject of politics in Vermont town
government. In the first place, he said, with 525 voters
(in the town of Danby) and only thirty town officers
to be elected, one would think that it would not be
necessary to elect one man to two offices. Not so, however, for two or three justices of the peace also serve
as selectmen. This means that, as holders of one office,
they count the ballots for the other, for which they
themselves are candidates. This struck the writer as not
wholly democratic. He had yet a second cause for com-
plaint: that the Republican candidates for justice of
the peace were nominated at a party caucus which was
so secret that he (the letter writer) had been unable

* ICP Case Series: No. 16, *Three Cases in Field Administration* (University of Alabama Press, 1953).

to find out when and where it was to be held, though as a Republican and prospective participant he had made a special effort to learn. The effect of this disclosure was so unpleasant, the writer continued, that when ". . . one of our town officers informed me that I had been appointed as assistant ballot-clerk for Tuesday's election, . . . I told him I wanted to accommodate a fellow I am working for who is building a barn" and so could not serve. What more graceful way to "take a walk" in rural Vermont?

A contemporary observer has written revealingly of politics in the conduct of the affairs of a rural irrigation district of the Far West.* The first three years of a recent five-year period, he reports, ". . . witnessed a county grand jury probe and indictment, a recall election, an outbreak of fisticuffs at a board session, numerous mass meetings, hirings, firings, charges and counter-charges. In the fourth year there were demands for reinstatement of a dismissed bookkeeper and accusations by him regarding the . . . holding of tea parties on district time, overcharges of a considerable number of water users, and negligence in the collection of . . . bills. Meanwhile his successor was jailed on the charge of grand theft. . . . Soon thereafter a recall was started against a director. . . . In the fifth year the manager was dismissed and the post filled on a temporary basis. . . ."

It is clear that the traditional concept of intimate, tranquil, personal, "non-political" little government by friends and neighbors, while an idyllic one, is not always or necessarily in accord with fact. The rural atmosphere is such, indeed, as to invite the familiar personal relationships which, whether so recognized or so

*John C. Bollens, *Special District Governments in the United States* (Berkeley: The University of California Press, 1957), Chapter 5, "Rural Districts."

called, form the essence of grass-roots political ties. Among larger units, the requirements of a budget, an accounting system, maintenance of detailed records, competitive purchasing, and (often) appointment by merit under civil service regulations tend to regularize and record these relationships. So does the lively competition of active political organizations, which makes access to public favor both more systematic and more difficult. There are relatively few trammels on political activity at the grass roots, where the lack of formal restraints is matched by the absence of personal inhibitions. The difference between politics in big government and politics in little government is largely quantitative in character: in kind, politics in rural government is pretty much like politics everywhere else. It may not be any worse in its consequences for democracy, generally speaking, but almost certainly it is no better.

In general summary, the shibboleths which surround the whole subject of rural government and democracy need to be called into question. Some of the more pervasive among them may be listed:

1. That frequent elections will result in a more democratic government than infrequent elections; that short terms of office will ensure a democratic system.

2. That the closer to the people a government is, the more democratic it is; that the popular election of many administrative officials, together with a frequent turnover in appointive officers, will bring about the desired closeness to the people and so will be conducive to democracy.

3. That a representative body elected by districts is more democratic than one whose members are elected at large.

4. That a representative chosen from a small district will more truly represent his constituency than one elected from a large district.

5. That a large legislative or governing body (for example, a county board) is more representative (that is, more democratic) than a small one.

6. That big politics is more subject to boss control and therefore is more to be feared than little politics.

7. That big government is (a) more impersonal and less human; (b) less subject to popular control; (c) more subject to political control; (d) more out of touch with local conditions; (e) less flexible; (f) more bureaucratic; and therefore and for all these reasons, (g) less democratic than grass-roots government.

These propositions, or some of them, may have been sound at one time, as indeed some (or all) may be valid now; but their validity is no longer to be granted without question. The assumption of the mantle of virtue in the name of grass-roots democracy has gone too long unchallenged. That there is much that is virtuous in rural government may be allowed, but a realistic appraisal places grass-roots performance at least a step this side of the perfection claimed for it by its more unrestrained admirers.

Virtually all who write and speak of democracy agree on the proposition that "government must be kept close to the people." Accepting this dictum, a question nevertheless must be raised as to how the desired end is to be accomplished. By what standards of measurement may government, or a given unit of government, be said to be close to or far from the people? What units and what organization shall be reckoned adequate to represent and to speak for the people? What are the procedures for bringing and keeping the government close to the people? Of equal importance is the question, how may government "close to the people" be made viable in operational terms? The nature of the challenge is clear enough: it is to contrive a system of rural government that will be able to render prompt

and energetic service without loss of responsibility to
or contact with the people, that will be both efficient
and democratic.

iv Grass Roots:
Perspective and Prospect

FROM THE RECORD it is clear
that there is a considerable gulf between the promise
of grass-roots philosophy and the performance of grass-
roots government. How may the philosophy be tem-
pered in the face of uncompromising reality? How may
practice be elevated through the challenge of high purpose? In what degree and through what measures may
the promise and the performance of grass-roots democracy be harmonized?

The World Around Us

It is necessary to observe in the beginning that the
foundation stone assumed for grass-roots democracy,
namely an agrarian way of life, is not in accord with
the facts which prevail in mid-twentieth century America. When Jefferson first began to expound his theory
of an agricultural democracy, the young nation was
95 per cent rural and only five per cent urban. The
rural-urban ratio remained almost unchanged for fifty
years: in 1840, 89 per cent of the population was still
rural, only eleven per cent urban. Beginning about the
middle of the century, however, a sharp decline in the
rural proportion of the population and a corresponding rise in the urban proportion set in; and this trend
has continued, though at a diminished rate since 1900.
In that year, sixty per cent of the population was rural,
forty per cent urban; by 1950, the proportion was al-

most exactly reversed, with 41 per cent reported as
rural, 59 per cent as urban. The most spectacular aspect of this trend is to be found in the rise of the
great cities; by 1950, nearly eighteen per cent of the
total population lived in urban centers of more than
500,000 population and almost thirty per cent lived in
cities of 100,000 or more.

Coincidental with the growth of the city has been
the rise of the labor union, which has increased in
membership strength from less than one million in
1900 to almost seventeen million in 1955. An announced
"favorite son" candidate for the Republican nomina-
tion for the Presidency in 1956 recently engaged in a
little "simple arithmetic" and came up with the conclusion that his party must carry the bulk of the work-
ingman vote if it wished to elect its candidates. "There
are more of them than any other type of individual,"
he explained. Thus have the "lower orders which in-
habit the cities" (de Tocqueville's characterization)
come to prominence on the political stage.

Not only has the rural population diminished as
the urban population has increased, but agriculture
has suffered a corresponding decline, in terms of numbers involved, at least. In 1910, the farm population
stood at just over 32 million, and in 1930 it still num-
bered 30.5 million. By 1950, however, it had dropped
to 25 million, and by 1953 to 22.7 million. The farm
population thus decreased more during the three years
1950-1953 than it had during the twenty years 1910-
1930. Further, the percentage loss was nothing short of
spectacular. In 1910, the farm population constituted
35 per cent of the total, but by 1953 the percentage
was only a little more than 14. In 1900, 35 per cent of
the total population was classified as rural farm; by
1950, the figure had declined to 18 per cent.

The data on farm employment are no less arresting.

In 1910, 13.5 million individuals were engaged in farm employment; by 1954, the number had dropped to less than 8.5 million. The proportion of the gainfully employed engaged in agricultural pursuits dropped from over 35 per cent in 1900 to about 15 per cent in 1950. In the latter year, the total of those engaged in agricultural pursuits ranked third in number among eleven major occupation groups (as reported by the United States Census).

The time has come to re-assess the place of agriculture in the public life of America. The farmers, and more especially the big farmers, continue to exercise a powerful influence on the course of public affairs. This is due partly to habit and tradition; partly to effective organization; partly to the farm bloc in Congress, which has much greater influence on legislation than sheer numbers would warrant; and partly to the independence of the farm vote (particularly in presidential elections), which keeps the big farm states, though normally Republican, from being regarded as "safe." It is due also, and in no small part, to the geographical basis of both our representative system and political party organization, which taken in combination ensures that simple numbers alone will not control. The advantage in numbers, however, has swung sharply to the city with its mass of industrial workers, and political influence ultimately must follow the population trend. There is emerging in America a new urban-industrial politics in which the place of agriculture must be radically modified. It may be, as a prominent geographer recently said, that ninety per cent of the world's immediate problems are rural, but that characterization is hardly applicable to mid-century America.

Within agriculture, some equally arresting trends may be discerned—trends which distinguish present-day agriculture sharply from that which prevailed even

half a century ago. The most striking of these grow
from the movement toward farm mechanization, which
is summarized in the simple facts that the number of
farm horses decreased from 21 million in 1910 to 5.3
million in 1950, while the number of farm automotive
vehicles increased from virtually none to an estimated
5.3 million passenger cars, 2.4 million trucks, and 3.3
million tractors. In 1910, farm machinery accounted
for only 3.1 per cent of the total value of farm assets;
by 1920 the proportion had increased to 4.6 per cent,
and by 1954 to 15.8 per cent. These figures, summary
though they be, point clearly to the progressively more
rapid mechanization of agriculture.

The process of farm mechanization has had three
immediately identifiable effects in terms of agricultural
technology. First, the agricultural revolution has
brought with it an ever-increasing measure of specialization, both as among farm units and within a given
unit. Farming has become a highly technical business,
a big farm nothing less than a food factory. Second,
agriculture has been drawn into the vortex of a complex industrial economy—to which, it is well to bear
in mind, its own contribution is constantly decreasing.
Third, the productivity of farm labor has increased
remarkably within the last few years. In 1940, twenty
per cent of the labor force was engaged in agriculture;
in 1955, thirteen per cent of the labor force produced
the second biggest crop in the nation's history, and
on the smallest acreage under cultivation in fifteen
years. The report of the Secretary of Agriculture for
1954 indicated that from 1947-1949 to 1954 the number
of man-hours worked on American farms declined
seventeen per cent while output per man-hour increased twenty per cent. Advances in farm mechanization were largely responsible for this dramatic increase
in farm labor productivity, the Secretary concluded.

In 1800, two farm laborers could produce enough food for themselves and one other person; now those same two laborers can raise enough to feed 38 people, and keep the whole crowd in tobacco besides. The technological revolution brought in its wake many momentous changes in agricultural practice. For one thing, the process of mechanization tended to favor the larger farm at the expense of the smaller, with the result that farm units have grown in size at an increasingly rapid rate in recent years. In 1949, 22 per cent of the farms were responsible for 73 per cent of the national agricultural produce. The other 78 per cent produced only 27 per cent of the total farm output and averaged only $1,440 in total receipts. The nation's farms were (and are) still predominantly small and unproductive; it is to these that mechanization will come last and in smallest measure.

Among the interesting effects of the United States Government's program of agricultural price supports is that on the one hand it has favored the large farmer, while on the other it has kept afloat many small farmers who otherwise would have been liquidated in the adjustment accompanying mechanization. Competition obviously is not taking its toll in the agricultural sector, largely because of government intervention to keep in business the farmer on the small and uneconomical unit. Speculation on the relations between the traditionally independent small farmer and his government is interesting in this context.

Another relationship which is in process of substantial modification is that between farm owner and farm tenant. In Jefferson's time, a farmer was almost always a farm owner; but farm ownership has been on the decline for decades, and farm tenancy has been on the rise. More and more farmers, therefore, work for other people. Stuart Chase has said (1944) that "a hundred

years ago sixteen out of every twenty Americans owned
their means of livelihood. Today seventeen out of
twenty do not." This represents a profound change in
the system of agriculture which Jefferson knew.

Still another significant change in agriculture practice is to be found in the increase in part-time farming.
This has occurred principally through industrial (or
other non-farm) employment among small farmers, and
through the rapid increase in farm ownership among
"hobby" farmers. The Bureau of Agricultural Economics estimated that there were 440,000 more part-
time and residential farms in 1945 than in 1930. The
Bureau further estimated that only about 4.3 of the
5.9 million Census farm units served as the primary
source of income for the farm family. Considering that
the small farms of the nation are concentrated in the
South and that such units are not subject to mechanization to the same degree as the larger farms, the effects
of the rapid industrialization of that region on agriculture are likely to prove quite dramatic.

The following tabulation presents five significant
agricultural trends in summary form.* There it may
be seen that, except for a dip in obeisance to the Great
Depression, the trends in farm power and machinery,
farm output, and real income per worker were uniformly upward from 1900 to 1949 but for a decline
of 25 per cent in real income from 1945 to 1949. At
the same time, the trend in farm employment was
uniformly downward throughout the period. The table
demonstrates anew that agriculture and agricultural
practice experienced revolutionary changes during the
first half of this century.

* Adapted from a table which appears in Sherman E. Johnson's,
"Technological Changes and the Future of Rural Life," *Journal of
Farm Economics*, XXXII, No. 2 (May, 1950), 225-239. The paragraphs
on the agricultural way of life also depend in part on the Johnson
article.

The farmer's way of life likewise has undergone profound changes in response to technological innovations. The drudgery of work has lessened both in the field and in the home, allowing more free time to the farmer and his family. Both real income and capital have increased, thus making it possible for farm families to buy automobiles, television sets, and electrical appliances "like other people." This has tended to close the gap between the level of living (or consumption)

Year	Farm Power and Machinery	Farm Employment	Farm Output	Farm Output per Worker	Real Income per Worker
1900	80	105	73	70	a
1910	105	111	79	71	88
1920	126	104	92	88	80
1930	118	102	95	93	76
1935-9	100	100	100	100	100
1940	106	97	110	113	102
1945	125	90	129	143	195
1949	164	90	138	153	150

aNot available

of farm families and the rest of the population. Rural people are less distinctive in dress, speech, and action than they were fifty or even 25 years ago. The old folks get around more, a larger percentage of the young ones go to college. Part of the increased farm income has gone into such institutions as improved schools and community recreation centers. Compared to the members of other occupational groups, the farmer, and particularly the small farmer, still does not live a life of luxury. His progress since 1900 nevertheless has been quite substantial, and the conditions under which he lives and works are much more favorable than they were fifty years ago.

The revolution in transportation has produced one

highly significant result which concerns the population as a whole and not only the farmer—the increasing mobility of the people. From 1940 to 1947, more than thirteen million people moved from one county to another within the same state, while twelve million moved across state lines. The Bureau of the Census remarked that ". . . probably never in the history of the United States has there been national population movement of such magnitude. . . ." During the year which ended with April, 1955, twenty per cent of the whole population changed their place of residence. The activity was least in the rural farm areas, but even there almost fifteen per cent of the people moved. This is a phenomenon peculiar to the automotive age; it is, as the Bureau of the Census says, without example in American history, though in the years to come it will not be reckoned unusual.

The world around us has assumed almost completely new contours in the last half-century. In the process of adaptation to the new imperatives, the agrarian way of life of the late 1800's disappeared from the American scene. The small farmer-owner gave way on the one hand to the large landowner and on the other to the farm tenant. The individualism of the frontier succumbed to the interdependence of an urban-industrial system as the farm family became more effectively assimilated to society. The simplicity of early rural life dissolved in the face of technological change, yielding to a specialized and vastly complex manner of existence. The common man is no longer the small frontier farmer he was in Jefferson's day, but an urban industrial worker instead.

What have these changes meant for government, especially for the little government of the branchhead community, for grass-roots democracy? Not a great deal, unhappily, and by any criterion not nearly enough.

The modifications in governmental structure seen in geographical adjustments (in the elimination of many smaller units, in particular) and in administrative reorganization have not been without significance, but they have been minuscule by comparison with the adaptations which the changed conditions require. It is notorious that social institutions respond tardily to the stimuli of technological advances, which do not require consensus among men for adoption. Institutional lag therefore is expected and understood. What cannot be so readily accepted is the continued rationalization of governmental structure and practice in nineteenth century terms. The cry for help comes from an urban-industrial democracy, but the answering voice is that of a wilderness agrarianism of a bygone day.

The Dilemmas of Democracy

Democracy is engaged in a continuing struggle to ameliorate the effects of certain basic dilemmas whose complete elimination seems impossible. Founded variously upon tradition, faith, hope, prejudice, conviction, dogma, momentum, or inertia (depending largely upon the predisposition of the viewer), they involve democracy in an incessant combat with the realities of emergent need. The reconciliation of these continuing conflicts is the permanent preoccupation of a democracy which is always striving but never quite achieving.

The most persistent and pervasive of these dilemmas is the rural-agrarian myth in counterposition to the urban-industrial reality. This dichotomy has been explored at sufficient length in the preceding section, and is mentioned here only by way of according it a proper place in the current context.

A second ever-present dilemma of democracy is found in the basic principle of equalitarianism in the face of obvious and observable differences, both individual and group. The fundamental rights are embodied in equality of opportunity and equality of treatment in the eyes of the law. Given a chance to achieve and the protection of the courts, an individual has little to fear at the hands of his fellow men; but these equalitarian rights are vitiated by conditions and practices which prevail on every hand. Prof. Lloyd Warner found a basic paradox between the democratic principle of equalitarianism and the observed reality of social and economic status in Jonesville.* He discovered in the city a system of social and economic strata defined in terms of family background, education, financial resources (kind as well as amount), church, clubs, kind and quality of dwelling, place of residence, and the like. He found, too, that people recognized and accepted status limits, and set themselves to the task of moving upward in the hierarchy.

It is the very fact that class lines in America are not impermeable that preserves the essence if not always the spirit of democracy. It is the possibility of moving upward (and downward), together with the fact that there is constant if limited mobility in both directions, that preserves an open society. The elimination of the right to strive and of the hope of reward in mobility would lead quickly to a monolithic society. Whether fascist or communist, the result would be the same for democracy. The dilemma is resolved, then, through preservation of the individual right of movement, that is, of opportunity, even though achievement is sometimes lamentably short of the ideal of equality.

Yet a third basic dilemma is posed by the unending contest between the whole and its parts. The parts are represented by the multiform economic-occupational-professional groups on the one hand and by the many

* W. Lloyd Warner, *Democracy in Jonesville* (New York: Harper & Brothers, 1949). This discussion rests in part upon Warner's analysis.

thousands of geographical districts and units on the other—and let it be recognized well that the fragmentation of attention, interest, capacity, and resources is equally real and equally damaging whether the part is represented by a local labor union or by a local unit of government. The effect is identical, for it eventuates in the identification of self-interest with the public interest and in the pleading of a special cause.

The whole is represented by the government—any government of competent jurisdiction with regard to a particular problem or issue. If a decision is to be made or action taken on a purely local matter, then a minor unit of government is (or may be) adequate to the need. If, however, the issue is of county-wide importance, then the government of the county alone is competent to take appropriate action; and no combination of minor governments or units within the county, not even the totality of all acting in unison, may properly lay claim to the jurisdiction which falls solely upon the government of the county itself. So for the government of the state where matters of state concern are at issue, and so for the federal government with regard to questions of national import.

At what level may government be expected to assume a general, public view with regard to large issues? Certainly not at the rural community level, for there the issues are generally local and therefore appropriate to community decision. The error lies not in encouragement of community action, but in encouragement of community action on matters which are of more than community import. Concerning these, a larger area is required—an area appropriate to the issue to be resolved. It is only as rural government is left behind, therefore, that the broad point of view necessary to the resolution of general problems can be expected to emerge; for the farther government (that is, govern-

mental officials, including elected representatives) is
from the grass roots, the broader the view it is likely to
adopt, the more general its concern, and the less strong
its marriage to local loyalties. Contrariwise, the closer
government is to the grass roots, the more preoccupied
it becomes with small concerns, the more engrossed in
details, the more myopic, and the narrower in view. At
the same time, the larger a government is, the more
complex is the problem of maintaining working relations with the people. This is not an unsolvable problem, but merely a difficult one. It is one aspect of the
continuing larger problem of harmonizing the needs
of the many special and partial publics with the over-
riding requirements of the whole public. Re-stated, the
problem is that of continuously reconciling local and
special needs to the demands of the public welfare.

A fourth of democracy's dilemmas grows from the
long tradition of weak and inanimate government in
the face of the growing need for an active and energetic one. The predilection clearly flows from the
American tradition of limited government, which in
turn is inseparable from the individualism of *laissez
faire*. To recognize the doctrinal strength of the tradition, however, is not to concede its validity in the cir-
cumstances which now prevail. Strong government has
risen step by step in response to overwhelming need,
and *laissez faire* has retreated not before the onslaught
of strong government but before the dire need for
energetic, indeed frequently for emergency, public action. The Interstate Commerce Commission, the Federal Trade Commission, and each of the great federal
regulatory agencies came into existence only after (a)
clear need for action had made itself felt, and (b) the
states had demonstrated their lack of capacity to take
effective action.

The predisposition of the people toward weak gov-

ernment extends also to a suspicion of strong leadership. Here is a further corollary dilemma, for on the
one hand strong government requires vigorous leadership, while on the other the executive head of the
government is the most faithful single repository of
representativeness for the whole of the people. This is
true in principle of any chief executive—county judge,
mayor, governor, president. Individual members of
legislative bodies represent at best but segments of the
population, at worst special interests or pressure groups.
Unhappily, the legislative body time and time again
has demonstrated its inability to rise above the personal
commitments, prejudices, and animosities of its individual members. The chief executive is in a position
to see things more nearly whole than are most of the
members of the legislative body, wherefore the responsibility of representing all the people falls most clearly
and most logically upon him. The chief executive may
not rise to the representative challenge of his office—
many have not; but the opportunity and the need for
leadership are there. Government at all levels needs
vigorous and imaginative leadership, not least because
of the representative character of the executive office.

A companion dilemma grows from the prevailing
myth of the beneficence of little government in the
face of the demonstrated incapacity of the bulk of the
minor units to discharge with satisfaction the services
required of government today. The fields in which
little government is competent to act grow more and
more restricted, with the result that government at the
grass roots is considerably less important with respect
to the totality of public action than it was half a century ago. Further, government grows larger with the
passing of the years. This is true of all government
except that classified here as grass-roots government,
which finds itself lagging farther and farther behind

the procession. The problem is not to defend rural
government against unfair attack by larger units, but
to reconcile vigorous government at each progressively
higher level with local initiative and responsibility and
a sense of participation. The problem is to bring big
government closer to the people, to build citizen interest in big government, to preserve (or inspire) popular confidence in big government, to interpret big
democracy to the people, to improve communication
and to reduce distance and remoteness. This is a difficult problem but it is not an impossible one, and even
if it were there would be no choice but to attempt its
solution. There is no escape from big government, because there is no escape from the conditions which
result in big government.

A dilemma as persistent as any that confronts democracy is that posed by the quarrel, continuing now
for well over a century, between the supporters of a
purely amateur corps of public employees and those
who insist that the public service must be professional-
ized. The historical protagonists are those who defend
the spoils system and those who advocate as an alternative the merit system. The former have lost ground
steadily for 75 years, during which "civil service" has
spread throughout the whole of our governmental structure, excepting principally the little governments at the
grass roots. Another kind of answer to the question
whether we shall be governed by amateurs or by pro-
fessionals is found in the scientific management movement, whose doctrines have been widely adapted to
public administration. The movements toward systematic fiscal administration and administrative reorganization, along with the recent emphasis on organization and methods, to illustrate, reflect the influence
of scientific management in a variety of ways. The
council-manager movement provides a striking instance

of the rejection of amateurism in favor of professionalism in one important segment of the public service.

A corollary aspect of this dilemma is found in the issue of the relative roles of generalist (amateur) and specialist (professional) in the process of governance. Members of legislative bodies along with the chief executive officers, it is generally agreed, must be persons of broad interests and competences. This is to say that they should be concerned rather with the determination of public policy than with its administration; in other words, they should be politicians. Virtually all employees of grass-roots governments answer this description. Excepting in the public schools, where even in the smaller districts at least some professional preparation is required, one must move upward into a fair-sized city or (normally) into a non-rural county before one will find technical competence a deciding factor in appointments to public office.

There is of course a role, and a vital role, for both generalist and specialist in the conduct of public affairs. The role of the generalist is to harmonize conflicting views and competing interests, to assist the people in arriving at consensus on public issues and to translate their will into effective governmental terms, to interpret the government to the people—in short, to serve as catalyst in arriving at public policy and as leader in making it effective. Technical proficiency is not expected of the generalist, of whom the principal attributes required are intelligence, a sensitivity toward government and its problems, an ability to synthesize, and a political sense or "feel." The specialist, on the other hand, must be familiar with the technical requirements of a particular job; for he enters upon the scene at the point where a program becomes an operation, and at this level of performance technical proficiency is paramount.

It is a prime task of administration to bridge the
gap between the generalist and the specialist, between
the politician and the professional man, between public
policy defined in general terms and program translated
into the specific acts of administration. The administrator, then, in a sense must be both generalist and
specialist, although in another and very important sense
he may be neither. He is required to be able to con-
ceive programs, to translate them into operational
terms, to grasp relationships, to deal with men. The
administrator not only organizes for and manages the
implementation of public policy, he translates and interprets that policy. He is therefore both a tool and an
exemplar of democracy.

To all but a handful of grass-roots governments, this
discussion of the relative roles of amateur and professional in government will be without point; for little
government, as has been observed, is the province almost exclusively of amateurs. It is one of the grave
weaknesses of grass-roots government, indeed, that it
has neither a sufficiently vigorous or varied program
nor the financial and human resources to make possible the specialization which the distinction made here
takes for granted.

One of the most debilitating dilemmas of American
public life grows from the almost universal observance
of ritual or form with only incidental regard for substance. The right of free speech as a long-accepted doctrine commands very wide public support, but its exercise is severely circumscribed. Freedom of belief, even
freedom of worship, basic components of the American
Creed for 180 years, are under severe attack, frequently
by those who are most voluble in defending the principles. Freedom of economic action becomes warped in
interpretation to the point where monopolies control
our economic life and individual opportunity vanishes.

The rights of the individual are strongly supported in public utterances, but conformity is enforced through economic and social circumstance. The tendency to insist upon allegiance to democratic or pseudo-democratic forms without reference to the experience of democratic living is almost universal.

The dilemmas of democracy rest upon a folklore which goes back to the time of Jefferson. They arise from the persistent manipulation of symbols, images, and myths which have little significant relation to the world around us. Such symbols provide impetus and give direction to progress, they serve important inspirational purposes, and in some sense they supply balance; but they also interpose obstacles to adaptation to changing conditions and needs. They depart farther and farther from reality with the passing of time, thus representing the original truth less and less perfectly. At the same time they tend to command ever greater strength and ever wider acceptance, partly because, since they have little to do with reality, no interest can be injured by protestation of platitude. In the end they become sacrosanct, having lost all substantive significance along the way. It was by this process that the grass roots came to be associated with everything good and virtuous in American life.

Gunnar Myrdal in *An American Dilemma* has proposed a suggestive reconciliation of America's ". . . high and uncompromising ideals and the spotty reality" of performance. He finds in this country an explicit body of national ideals which are ". . . more widely understood and appreciated than similar ideals . . . anywhere else." These ideals are embraced by almost everyone in American society. If they suffer in the process of translation into a way of life, the nation has still profited measurably through having professed them. The American Creed therefore serves a noble purpose as a statement of the national standard by which performance is to be measured, as a delineation of distant goals toward which the nation is constantly adjured. It is better to steer toward a light, however distant, than to steer in total darkness. It is only when the light becomes a will-o'-the-wisp that its worth comes into question. The seeming light appears sometimes to have this character with respect to broad areas of grass-roots government in America.

The Climate of Democracy

Democracy is an exceedingly difficult term to define. It is in such common use and is so firmly embedded in the national vocabulary that every American knows what the term means—at least, he knows what *he* means when he employs it. Depending on context, he means the three-point program announced by the old-line candidate for county commissioner: social security, the right to say what he pleases so long as he does not start a riot, the forty-hour work week, price support for tobacco, or a tariff on English-built bicycles. He means, in short, the things which go on about him, things with which he is familiar and which affect his daily life. He is likely to think of his government, which he assumes to be democratic, in terms both of what it does for him and how it does it. He does not distinguish between democracy as ends and democracy as means.

Here democracy is taken to mean a system in which the individual has the controlling voice in determining the goals of the state and the ways by which those goals are to be sought. The determination of goals has to do with policy, the determination of ways with administration; but both center on means rather than ends. Worthy ends—the public good, the general welfare—may be assumed for a democratic polity, but they may not be specified as to content. For worthy ends are not the exclusive preserve of democracy. Franco's Spain and Mao's China have many announced goals which do not differ appreciably from those to which we aspire; yet few in America would suppose those states to be democratic, notwithstanding their appropriation of much of the superficial paraphernalia of democracy. Spain and China are not democratic by American standards not because their announced goals are not worthy but because their methods of operation do not accord a proper place to the individual. Their ends in some particulars are harmonious with American ideals, but their methods are abhorrent.

The essence of democracy, then, is to be found in means employed, not in ends sought. It is a way of life, whose value is to be judged by the manner of conduct of public affairs. Such conduct is not subject to quantitative analysis, but may be said rather to grow from a pervasive *climate*. The climate of democratic government cannot be precisely delineated in terms of temperature, humidity, precipitation, and prevailing winds, but its characteristic features lend themselves to description in general terms.

The climate of democracy may be defined first in terms of elections, for here is where the elective officers of government offer themselves and their records for periodic accounting, and here is where the people most manifestly bring their influence to bear. Open and free elections, held at stated intervals and with reasonable frequency, provide the foundation for the democratic process. With popular elections, democracy may prevail; without them, it surely cannot.

A second element which enters into the climate of democracy concerns the character of the contests for public office. If the contests are real rather than rigged, and if candidates present themselves in sufficient numbers to permit the voters reasonable choice, then the entity has taken a second long step toward the achievement of democracy.

A third criterion is to be found in the nature of the campaign which precedes the election. It must cover a period long enough to allow the issues and the candidates to be adequately presented yet short enough to ensure sustained voter interest; the issues must be discussed freely and fully, and the candidacies must be related to the issues. The campaign, in short, must be meaningful.

Next, the services performed by the unit must be sufficiently broad and varied to give its activities substantial public consequence. If the government does little or nothing of interest or significance, if the stakes which are presented to the voter at election time are negligible, then both campaign and election are likely to be without significance and the public without interest. There is no more effective deterrent to vitality in democracy than the hollow observance of routine procedures.

Not only must the business of the government have some intrinsic significance, but the issues presented must be significant in terms of policy. They must be important issues and they must be defined in such fashion as to assume meaning within the experience, needs, and interests of the voters. Issues presented in terms of a local party row, for example, excite nobody, except perhaps the principal participants. The issues of a campaign can produce a challenge, they can lead to citizen excitement, or they can lead to utter boredom. If the electoral process is to be meaningful, important issues must be presented for citizen action. Further, the outcome of the election must be uncertain, otherwise issues will be spurious and candidacies unreal. What the people do must affect the result, else the whole election procedure is make-believe.

Finally, the nature and extent of popular participation in the process of governance affords a significant criterion. It is, of course, important to know whether the voters rise to the issues of a campaign, whether they participate in the campaign and if so in what ways, whether they attend and take part in political meetings, whether on occasion they announce for public office, and to what extent they go to the polls and vote on election day. In a sense, however, these questions are secondary, however important. To attribute the supposed decadence of democracy to voter apathy, as is done regularly by most speakers and by many writers on democracy, is to mistake effect for cause. The quiescence of the voters is not a cause of the fancied decline of democracy, but a result. The cause is more deep-seated and much less evident. It is to be found in the routine observance of democratic forms from which, too often, substance and spirit have fled. *Pro forma* elections, hollow campaigns, manufactured issues, artifical candidacies—this is the world of make-believe democracy in which the citizen is expected to accept fantasy as fact. That he refuses to do this, and that oftentimes he "takes a walk" on election day, is to be attributed more to his good judgment than to his apathy. He fails to vote not because he is delinquent but because politics, and more largely government, has ceased to have significant meaning for him.

It is unhappily true that the conditions of government in rural America are less hospitable to the development of a favorable climate of democracy than are those which prevail in other environments. The principal reason is that little government does not have the substance to support a system which is or which can be really democratic. Rural government is "close to the people," it is easy and personal and informal and intimate in procedure and relatively simple in organization; but it has little magic to stir men's minds. It is too picayune, too narrow in outlook, too limited in horizon, too self-centered in interests, to challenge the imagination or to enlist the support of the voter. Grass-roots government is, in fine, too small to be truly democratic.

The Agenda of Democracy

Jeremy Bentham employed the phrase "The Agenda of the State" to refer to those things which must be kept in mind if a vital community is to be maintained. Similarly democracy may be said to have an agenda, comprising a number of areas where problems are central to the strength of the democratic process and continuing in character, and where solutions are never final. Each man may draw up his own agenda. That which follows centers on the problem areas which have been discovered in the operation of democracy at the grass roots.

First, the superstructure of rural government—the units by which the affairs of government are conducted at the grass roots—is deserving of continuing consideration. There is little organized knowledge of the services performed by small governments, or of their resources, or of their relations with other governments. Trends in the domain of little government, which in numbers employed, revenues and expenditures, indebtedness, and the other tangible measures of governmental activity, are of comparatively little importance, have escaped systematic treatment. Yet if Jefferson's theories of agrarian democracy are to provide the framework for thinking about democracy in modern America, and if grass-roots government is the legatee of Jeffersonian agrarianism, then it behooves us to know more about little government than the facts now available permit us to know.

There have been many studies of bureaucracy in the last quarter-century, but no systematic inquiry into rural bureaucracy. The nature of rural bureaucracy, its scope and size, its internal relations and its relations with the people; the significance of part-time and amateur service; the respective domains, potential as well as actual, of generalist and specialist; the role and the promise of expertise, all with reference to the conditions of public employment in rural government, are suggestive of the subjects worthy of exploration.

The field of politics commands an expanding literature, yet little attention has been focused on the political process at the grass roots. It has been easy, and in view of our agrarian heritage natural, to assume that all is well with politics at the branchhead; and this almost uniformly has been the way taken by researchers and writers. The result has been a heavy emphasis on urban politics, and particularly on urban machines and bosses and bossism, at the expense of a meaningful body of data about rural politics. The nature of the local political organization and its role in state and national politics, political leadership, issues, campaign methods, the sources of campaign funds, the administration of elections, the rewards of office, citizen participation— here are some aspects of grass-roots politics worthy of much more consideration than they have had in the past.

The problem of popular representation and the nature of representative government requires continuing attention, for nowhere is terminology more loosely employed or meaning more vague than in discussions of representation. Particularly is this true when the conversation turns to rural government, of which it is assumed that, if there are enough units and they are small enough—if, that is, government is "close enough to the people"—the problem of representation will take

care of itself. Despite this widespread conviction, which
goes back to the beginnings of responsible government
in this country, some fundamental questions are justi-
fied regarding the representativeness of grass-roots institutions. What is the relation between representativeness and: the size of and services rendered by the unit?
the size of the election district? the size, frequency of
meeting, and manner of organization of the representative body? the qualifications required of, the length
of term served by, and the compensation paid to the
representative? the private-life employment of the representative? the activities of pressure groups? In fine,
in what sense may the organs of rural government be
said to be representative, and wherein do they fall short?
How successful is government in the New England
town or the southern rural county in arriving at a
satisfactory definition of public policy and translating
it into action? There are, of course, ready answers to
these questions and others like them, but few or none
based on objective analysis.

The nature and significance of provincialism has
received too little attention in terms appropriate to an
analysis of rural democracy. The easy assumption is
that the basic problem is to determine grass-roots sentiment, which then somehow will be transmuted into
the general will, and thence into action cast in terms
of the public welfare. This clearly is not what happens.
What does happen and how it happens are matters
worthy of much more attention than they have received.
The reconciliation of local with larger interests, the
harmonization of narrow with broad concerns, the soft-
ening of parochial preoccupations in the face of the
general need: this is a subject deserving of our best
thought, partly because to date it has received little
systematic attention.

Symbolism plays a role in American democracy as

yet but little apprehended. A hope, a desire, a wish receives hortatory statement which moves by easy stages from hypothesis to theory; the theory over the course of the years acquires the status of a tradition, which by a process of imperceptible sclerosis becomes a dogma which may be questioned only at peril. Simultaneously a structure of symbolism comes into being which is designed to support and procure unquestioning allegiance to the dogma. The symbolism takes form in an extravagant and unreal vocabulary which in the end divorces the dogma from observable fact. Thus a student of the institution finds it necessary to preface his conclusion that town government in New England is dying for want of citizen interest with the statement that town government is a tower of strength to local democracy in New England. Much of our symbolism represents a degeneration of the American Creed as identified by Gunnar Myrdal. The relationship between tradition, symbolism, and the practice of rural democracy is worthy of close and continuing scrutiny.

In another direction, the program (or action) implications of the commitment to rural democracy, more especially on the part of state and federal agencies, are deserving of further exploration. Philip Selznick has pointed out that the assimilation of local elements into a non-local program may have certain "unanticipated consequences" in terms both of organization and of program. Taking the case of the TVA, he argues that the program developed by that agency over the years is not one which a thoughtful reader of the TVA Act of 1933 might have anticipated. Further, he continues, neither the present organization nor the method of operation of TVA could have been foreseen from its origin and early history. These unanticipated developments Selznick attributes to TVA's decision to "co-opt" local units and agencies by drawing them into the

TVA orbit as collaborators, a decision which necessitated some major compromises and countless minor ones. Not all would embrace this thesis—David Lilienthal assuredly would not—but certainly it is worthy of careful analysis by students of grass-roots democracy.

The relationship between stability and flexibility within the framework of democratic practice is a subject of continuing concern. To survive in a changing world, government must be ready and able to adapt its machinery and procedures to the requirements of new conditions. The federal government generally has been responsive to new demands: the Constitution has proved sufficiently flexible and the administrative structure by and large has responded satisfactorily to the changing character of society. The states have proved somewhat less adaptable, partly through more rigid constitutions, partly because of their more limited jurisdictions, and partly because of their frequently narrower outlook. The units of local government have proved less flexible still, for there it is extremely difficult to effect significant changes in governmental organization and practice. Government at the grass roots is particularly and peculiarly impervious to change. If the capacity to respond to changing conditions is an attribute of a vital democracy, then it may be argued that grass-roots government is less democratic than that of either the nation or the states.

A companion problem has to do with the methods by which change in governmental organization and practice may be brought about. Students of government have been in almost unanimous agreement for half a century that there are a great many more counties than are needed to carry on the work of county government; yet during that period not more than a dozen counties have been eliminated. New England furnishes many examples of towns which are no more than hollow shells; Vermont, for example, has 238 towns, some of which exist as legal entities only; but in the last twenty years only two Vermont towns have been abolished. The annals of government are filled with such anachronisms, so that any citation of example is of necessity invidious. Technological change is no respecter of tradition, but comes when it will without benefit of referendum. Why must the institutions of government, whose prime duty it is to cope with the expanding technology in behalf of the people, be in so many respects fifty years behind their quarry? Consideration of this problem involves contemplation of the role of custom, tradition, folkways, and mythology, of the ways of group life, of the stakes involved and the parties at interest, of the role of adversity and hard times—in short, of all the factors which affect group reaction to change. Approached positively, the problem is one of effecting the modifications in governmental organization and practice necessitated (or made desirable) by changing conditions. Considerable progress has been made in this area in recent years both through the contributions of the anthropologists and social psychologists and through increased attention to what has come to be called "technical assistance." Much of study and analysis remains to be done, however, for we still know distressingly little about how change is wrought in government.

Finally, it may be noted that the problem of institutional adaptation, along with a number of the others here identified, is not less administrative than political in character. Indeed these essays in their entirety implicitly recognize the joint sovereignty of politics and administration over the field of rural government. Politics (as, essentially, the determination of public policy) remains paramount; but the process of governance is a continuum, as Paul Appleby has observed, to which the administrative contribution is vital. Policy and administration appear therefore as the two edges of a sword. If there is no worthwhile polity except one democratic in spirit, there is no vigorous democracy except one administratively effective. Wherefore the role of administration in government is commended as an abiding concern for all who would see democracy prevail.

Index